✱ ✱ ✱ Kid ✱ ✱ ✱
Authors

TRUE TALES OF CHILDHOOD FROM

✱ FAMOUS WRITERS ✱

STORIES BY *DAVID STABLER*   ILLUSTRATIONS BY *DOOGIE HORNER*

Library of Congress Cataloging in Publication Number: 2016961075

ISBN: 978-1-59474-987-2

Printed in China

Typeset in Bell, Bulmer, Franklin Gothic, and Linowrite

Illustrations by Doogie Horner
Illustration coloring by Mario Zucca
Production management by John J. McGurk

Quirk Books
215 Church Street
Philadelphia, PA 19106
quirkbooks.com

10 9 8 7 6 5 4 3 2 1

J.K. ROWLING

STAN LEE   EDGAR ALLAN POE   ZORA NEALE HURSTON

Kid
Authors

TRUE TALES OF CHILDHOOD FROM

FAMOUS WRITERS

STORIES BY *DAVID STABLER*   ILLUSTRATIONS BY *DOOGIE HORNER*

ROALD DAHL   LANGSTON HUGHES   LUCY MAUD MONTGOMERY   MARK TWAIN

Table of Contents

PART THREE

The Write Stuff

Introduction

Everybody loves a good story—and we all know that a well-told story has a beginning, a middle, and an end. This is a book about how the stories of sixteen famous authors began.

Some of them knew from very early on that they were going to be writers. Edgar Allan Poe, the legendary author of "The Raven" and "The Tell-Tale Heart," used to recite poetry and dress up as a ghost to frighten grown-ups at parties.

EN GARDE!

And the poet Langston Hughes spent hours in his local library, reading collections of mythology, verse, and African American history.

Other kid authors had to overcome obstacles on the road to success. Laura Ingalls Wilder, the writer of *Little House on the Prairie*, grew up on the frontier, where she faced harsh winters and attacks by locusts.

And then there is J. K. Rowling. Long before she wrote the best-selling Harry Potter novels, she was just another kid in middle school trying to make decent grades and fend off bullies. Believe it or not, she often found herself getting into fights! She took comfort in writing stories about feisty heroines who fought back against evil villains.

And finally we have Jeff Kinney, whose most formidable foes were his three siblings. Every morning, Jeff and his siblings found themselves in a heated competition to determine who would use the bathroom first. Jeff took the "wimpy moments" of his childhood and turned them into *Diary of a Wimpy Kid*, one of the most successful children's book series of all time.

We all have a story to tell, and whether or not you grow up to become a great writer, all those stories start in the same place: childhood. Some kids are born story-tellers, others learned to take their unique experiences and turn them into tales that would entertain and inspire. We know how their stories ended, but how much do you really know about how their stories *began?* We're going back to the beginning to find out!

IT'S NOT EASY BEING A KID

BULLIES,
MEAN TEACHERS,
EVEN *BABOON SPIDERS!*

———— THESE ————

Kid Authors

FACED
(AND DEFEATED)
ALL KINDS OF
PROBLEMS.

J. R. R. TOLKIEN

Meets a Baboon Tarantula

J. R. R. Tolkien's classic tales *The Hobbit* and *The Lord of the Rings* take place in a magical, make-believe realm called Middle-earth. But the author found inspiration in one of the real-life places where he grew up—the dusty plains of South Africa—not to mention his unlucky encounter with one of the world's deadliest insects.

It started with a monkey invasion, continued with a baby kidnapping, and ended with a spider attack. J. R. R. Tolkien's time in South Africa was brief, but it left him with vivid memories to last a lifetime.

If you've ever read *The Lord of the Rings*, you may know about Shelob, the giant evil spider who guards the entrance to Mordor. But did you know there was a *real* spider in Tolkien's life—and that it nearly put an end to the great storyteller's career before it even began?

John Ronald Reuel Tolkien—or Ronald, as he was called—was born in Bloemfontein, the capital of the South African province then known as the Orange Free State. But Ronald always thought of himself as English. His parents, Arthur and Mabel Tolkien, had moved to

South Africa from England only the year before, after Arthur got a job at a bank.

Ronald's father was often away on business, leaving his son in the care of his mother and servants. The first summer Ronald spent in his new hometown was one of the hottest that anyone could remember. As a baby, Ronald had to wear frilly white dresses—called pinafores—to keep cool. In letters to relatives, his mother boasted that he looked like an elf or a fairy.

Even worse than the heat were the bugs and beasts. Flies buzzed about constantly, and locusts devoured crops in the fields. A family of wild monkeys lived next door. One day, a monkey vaulted the fence and rampaged through the Tolkiens' garden, shredding three of Ronald's pinafores hanging on the clothesline.

Then, to make matters even worse, baby Ronald got kidnapped!

Well, sort of. Some might say he was just "borrowed" for a while. Apparently, a servant named Isaak was so taken by the adorable Tolkien infant that he took Ronald to show him to the people of his village.

After spending the night with Isaak and his family, Ronald was back in his crib the next morning, unharmed. Although he always claimed he had no memory of the incident, as an adult, J. R. R. Tolkien often wrote about characters who get captured or kidnapped.

One childhood memory did stick with Ronald forever. You could even say that it left quite an impression on him . . . with its *teeth*.

One very hot summer day, as he was just learning to

walk, Ronald was strolling through the garden when he stumbled on a hairy, black, eight-legged creature the size of a dinner plate. Ronald had no idea what it was, but it looked mean. He would later learn that it was called the Hercules Baboon Tarantula and it was one of the largest, heaviest, and rarest spiders in the world.

Baboon tarantulas are usually not aggressive, but they will defend themselves if they feel threatened—as Ronald soon found out. In his haste to back away, he startled the critter. It scuttled forward and bit him on the foot.

"Owwww!" Ronald cried, wincing in pain. It felt as if his foot was on fire. Shrieking, he took off running into the high grass. Lucky for him, his nurse was nearby. When she realized what had happened, she scooped up Ronald into her arms. "Tarantula!" she shouted, and then she took her first good look at the itchy red mark the spider had left behind.

The nurse lay Ronald on the ground. To help him, she lifted his leg and placed his swollen foot in her mouth, sucking out the spider venom. When she had drained the wound of the poison, she threw Ronald over her shoulder and carried him, like a sack full of flour, back home to his mother.

I'M NOT LOOKING FORWARD TO THIS EITHER, YOU KNOW.

"Mrs. Tolkien! Mrs. Tolkien!" she called out as she entered the house. "A tarantula bit your son!"

When Mabel Tolkien saw the welt on her son's foot, she took him from the nurse's arms and asked Isaak to fetch some bandages and lotion. After the wound was dressed, Ronald began to tell her the full story of what had happened. "It was a spider as big as a dragon!" he reported. And for the rest of his life, he would always be terrified of spiders.

One day a few years later, after Ronald's family had moved back to England, he was sitting by himself dreaming up characters for the first story he would ever write. He immediately imagined the most fearsome creature he could think of: a dragon. But in his mind, he may have been picturing a different kind of creature altogether—a critter like the one that had frightened him out of his wits that summer afternoon in South Africa. Ronald didn't remember all the details of that fateful day, but he never forgot what it felt like to run scared through the high, dry grass.

J. K. ROWLING

A Storybook Life

She created the amazing character Harry Potter, but her time in school was anything but magical. J. K. Rowling had to fend off a bully, defy the low expectations of her teachers, and overcome her own shyness on the way to becoming one of the world's most famous authors.

One summer day in 1990, a 24-year-old aspiring writer named Joanne Rowling found herself stuck for four hours on a train bound for London. As she gazed out the window, an idea for a new character popped into her head. He was a boy wizard, and though she didn't yet have a name for him, she knew just what he looked like and exactly what kind of enchanted school he would attend.

Sometimes the best ideas come in a flash, like magic. It took six years for Jo—who now called herself J. K. Rowling—to write the first Harry Potter adventure. When the book was finally published, it made the author an overnight sensation.

J. K. Rowling's life also began with a rail trip, in a manner of speaking. Her parents met on a train traveling north from England to Scotland in the winter of 1964. It was love at first sight, and they were married the following spring. Jo was born on the last day of July in 1965.

Jo's father, Peter Rowling, managed an aircraft factory. Her mother, Ann, worked in a laboratory. They began reading to their daughter when she was very young. One of Jo's first memories is of her father reading to her from *The Wind in the Willows* by Kenneth Grahame. Jo had measles at the time, but even as an adult she still remembers the characters from the book: Mole, Mr. Badger, Ratty, Toad of Toad Hall, and all the others.

When Jo was almost two years old, her mother gave birth to another baby, a girl named Dianne. To keep Jo occupied while her sister was being born, Jo's father gave her a ball of Play-Doh. Even years later, Jo still has a vivid memory of "eating the Play-Doh" while her sister was being delivered.

During their childhood, Jo and Di were constant companions. They loved to play games together, especially involving make-believe. Their favorite was called the "cliff game." Jo would grab hold of the top step of their staircase and hang on as though she was about to fall off a cliff. Then she'd plead with Di to rescue her before she plummeted down the steps.

Di never did. Time and again, Jo let go and plunged to the floor below. Then it was her sister Di's turn to hang off the cliff.

Jo and Di also liked to make up stories, mostly about rabbits. The sisters desperately wanted a pet rabbit of their own. They even named their dog Thumper, after the rabbit in the Disney movie *Bambi*. But they could never catch a bunny to bring home with them.

Instead, Jo made up fantasy stories, which she read aloud to her sister. In one story, Di fell down a rabbit hole, where a family of bunnies gave her strawberries to eat.

Di loved hearing her sister tell stories and begged Jo to retell them over and over. To help remember them, Jo started to write them down. The first story she ever set to paper was about a rabbit called Rabbit who caught the measles. While sick, he was visited by his friends, including a giant bee named Miss Bee.

At age seven, Jo wrote her first adventure story, an action-packed thriller called "The Seven Cursed Diamonds." It wasn't her best effort, but as she continued to imagine new stories, Jo began to think that she would like to be a writer someday. She didn't tell anyone for fear they would dismiss her dream. She thought her stories were not yet good enough.

Around this time, Jo and Di became friends with a brother and sister who would provide the inspiration for Jo's most famous character. Ian and Vikki Potter lived down the street from the Rowlings in the village of Winterbourne. At Jo's suggestion, the four friends dressed up and played Witches and Wizards. Ian would don fake eyeglasses and his father's long coat to portray the wizard, while Jo made up spells and potions for the three girl witches to cast.

Something about Ian's costume—and his distinctive last name—stuck in Jo's mind. She would return to them later . . .

When Jo was nine, her family moved to a new home in a tiny town in the English countryside. The ancient village of Tutshill was home to a real castle that dated back to medieval times, many centuries ago. Inside was what people believed to be the oldest toilet in Britain.

Just a short walk from their house was a forest where Jo drew inspiration for her imagined adventures. "My mother used to give me a sandwich and a drink and I'd be in the forest until nightfall," Jo recalled.

In the fall, Jo enrolled in Tutshill Primary School. It's never easy being the new kid, but for Jo it was especially hard. If Jo thought that her talent for story-telling would make her popular, she was about to learn that the opposite was true.

On the first day of school, Jo met her new teacher: a

short, severe-looking woman named Mrs. Morgan. She instantly struck fear in Jo's heart by handing out an arithmetic test—math was Jo's worst subject. Even more frightening, the quiz was full of questions about fractions, which Jo had not yet learned. Despite giving her best effort, Jo scored a zero.

After grading the test, Mrs. Morgan instructed Jo to sit in the far right row of desks.

This, Jo discovered, was the "stupid row," where the teacher put her poorest-performing students. The "clever" kids sat on the left. "I was as far right as you could get without sitting in the playground," Jo later remembered. But Jo worked hard and finally earned a promotion to one of the left-hand rows.

Jo's difficulty fitting in continued in middle school;

she later described her younger self as "quiet, freckly, short-sighted, and rubbish at sports." Jo arrived at Wyedean School expecting the worst. She had heard a rumor that on the first day of class, the older students would dunk the head of a new arrival down the toilet— and then flush it. That never happened to Jo, but she did have to confront a bully for the first time.

Although Jo didn't start the fight, she refused to back down when the other girl started punching her. For a few days, Jo became a hero among the other students for standing up to her tormentor. But Jo knew the truth. The only reason she hadn't gotten flattened was because her locker held her up, like a human punching bag. She spent the next several weeks peering around every corner in case the bully was waiting to ambush her.

Eventually, Jo found a better way to deal with her problems at school. Instead of battling bullies, she began writing about feisty heroines who fight back against evil villains. She made friends with other quiet, shy kids, and together they spent their lunchtime telling long stories that, Jo recalled, "usually involved us all doing heroic and daring deeds we certainly wouldn't have done in real life."

AND THE RABBIT ASKED HER, "WOULD YOU LIKE MORE BERRIES?"

As she got older, Jo grew less quiet and less shy. She ditched her glasses and started wearing contact lenses, which made her less scared of being punched in the face. She began to excel at her English and foreign language classes, although math and science remained a challenge. Her chemistry teacher described her as "a daydreamer who never answered questions about science and hated taking part in experiments." (Jo later got her "revenge" by making him the model for Severus Snape, the sinister Professor of Potions at Hogwarts School of Witchcraft and Wizardry.)

MISS ROWLING...

By Jo's final year of middle school, she was widely regarded as one of the smartest and most capable students at Wyedean. The teachers voted her Head Girl, a kind of class president. When dignitaries visited, it was Jo's job to show them around. She was also in charge of organizing school assemblies. Jo said later that she based the character of intelligent, resourceful Hermione Granger on herself during this period.

Although Jo's school days were difficult, they did prepare her for the challenges she faced as an adult. As a single mom, she struggled to pay her bills and get her literary career off the ground. She spent many afternoons writing in coffee shops while her baby daughter slept in a stroller beside her. But she persevered because she had faith in the power of her imagination.

In 2001, after she won worldwide fame as the creator of Harry Potter, J. K. Rowling returned to Tutshill Primary for a visit. She was hailed as the school's greatest living graduate. In July 2006, the Wyedean School library was dedicated in her honor. Her storybook life at last had a happy ending.

EDGAR ALLAN POE

Little Orphan Edgar

Edgar Allan Poe was a master of the scary story, featuring sinister animals, hauntings, and other horrors. But the supernatural chills he described in his fictional works and poetry were nothing compared to the real-life frights he survived during his difficult and sometimes lonely childhood.

"**From childhood's hour** I have not been as others were," Edgar Allan Poe once wrote. But if this orphan son of traveling actors had not been so unusual as a child, would he have grown up to become the author of such macabre masterpieces as "The Raven" and "The Tell-Tale Heart"?

Edgar Poe was born on January 19, 1809, in Boston, Massachusetts. He had two siblings, an older brother named William and a younger sister named Rosalie. His parents, David and Elizabeth Arnold Hopkins Poe, were stage actors whose busy performance schedule took them out of town for long periods.

IF ONLY EDGAR WERE HERE, MY JOY WOULD BE COMPLETE.

BRAVO!

BRAVO!

ENCORE!

While they were away from home, the Poes often left Edgar in the care of his grandparents in Baltimore. Other times he stayed with an elderly nursemaid.

When Edgar was just two years old, his father abandoned the family and disappeared from his life forever. Some say that David Poe was distraught over all the bad reviews he received as an actor. He died a short time later.

That was only the beginning of Edgar's misfortunes. In the fall of 1811, his mother died of tuberculosis. The three Poe children were now orphans. A call went out for foster parents willing to raise them. William went to live with his grandparents. Rosalie was adopted by a Scottish family, the Mackenzies. And Edgar was taken in by John Allan, a prosperous Virginia merchant, and his wife, Frances.

Edgar soon moved into his new home above John Allan's store on a corner of Main Street in Richmond. He added his foster father's last name to his own, calling himself Edgar Allan Poe.

John Allan had also been orphaned as a child and was determined to give Edgar every advantage in life. Frances Allan, Edgar's new foster mother, also doted on him. She styled Edgar's hair in curls and dressed him up like a boy prince.

In the evenings, the Allans threw lavish parties during which they encouraged Edgar to entertain their guests. Eager to please his new family, Edgar would stand in front of the assembled throng and recite famous poems from memory. Or he would climb onto the living room table, raise a glass, and toast the health of the partygoers in a grand, theatrical manner.

The Allans were enthralled by Edgar's dramatic performances. But there was a downside to all the adoration they showered upon him. In time, Edgar grew spoiled and began to think he could get away with anything. One time his teacher caught him misbehaving and sent him home with a rotten vegetable hung around his neck as punishment. John Allan was furious. He criticized the teacher for humiliating his son and threatened to withdraw Edgar from school.

The only people in the Allan household who didn't treat Edgar like royalty were the servants. At night he liked to head over to their quarters, where they would gather to share ghost stories around a roaring fire. The tales of ghouls in graveyards left a permanent impression on Edgar. Once, when he was returning home from a trip to the post office, the horse he was riding passed by a cemetery. Edgar became gripped by fear. "They will run after us and drag me down!" he shrieked, as if a shambling horde of zombies was about to snatch him from his saddle.

During this time, Edgar also became terrified of the dark. He was convinced that he would wake up in the night to find a monster in his bed. To protect himself, he would draw the sheets around his head so tight that he nearly suffocated.

However much his fears plagued him, Edgar was keen for everyone to know that he was no scaredy-cat. When, in 1815, the Allans sailed for Great Britain, where John Allan hoped to pursue a new business opportunity, Edgar hopped onto the dock at Liverpool begging his foster father to tell everyone within earshot that he had not been frightened during the journey across the ocean.

The Allans spent five years in England, where Edgar studied Latin and Greek, horticulture, and mathematics. He even took dance lessons.

When the family returned to Virginia, Edgar was much better educated than most of his classmates. Also by this time, he had begun writing poetry. One of his early verses will sound familiar to anyone who has read his later poem "The Raven":

Last night, with many cares & toils oppress'd,
Weary, I laid me on a couch to rest.

HMMM...

Pretty soon, Edgar had compiled enough poems to fill a book. John Allan showed Edgar's manuscript to the headmaster at his son's new school, but the headmaster advised against trying to publish it. The poems were too good, he said, and he worried that the adulation would go to Edgar's head, which was already swelled enough.

Edgar was doing well with his schoolwork, but not so well with his new schoolmates. When the other boys found out that he lived with foster parents, they shied away. Although Edgar tried to lead the other kids in pranks and games, many refused to follow. Edgar took these slights to heart. At the end of each school day, he gathered up his belongings and headed for home by himself. He never asked any of his classmates to come and play with him. Sometimes he went on long, solitary walks in the woods outside of town.

For a long time, Edgar didn't even try to fit in. He became notorious for playing mischievous practical jokes. Once, when a boy and his sister came over to spend Christmas with the Allans, Edgar took delight in tormenting the girl with a toy snake. He poked her with it until she ran away in terror.

As an outsider, Edgar was also a target for bullies. When he was fourteen years old, he got into a fight with a classmate. The other boy was much larger and quickly gained the advantage, pummeling Edgar in the face and head. Suddenly, Edgar turned the tables on his opponent and began clocking him into submission.

"I was just waiting for him to lose his breath!" Edgar exclaimed. After that episode, kids learned not to mess with the little poet. But he still had a hard time making friends.

Though it took a while, eventually Edgar did win over his classmates. No one is sure exactly when he turned the situation in his favor. Maybe it was the day he saved a boy from drowning. Granted, Edgar had thrown the boy into the water in the first place, but he quickly decided that now was not the time for jokes. Edgar—who was an excellent swimmer—chose to dive in and rescue the boy before it was too late.

Edgar earned another measure of respect on one hot June day when, on a bet, he swam a six-mile stretch of the James River. Upon emerging from the water, his neck, face, and back were blistered from the blazing sun. But Edgar wasn't tired, despite swimming against a roaring tide. In fact, immediately after completing the feat, he walked the six miles back to town!

In time, people started to appreciate Edgar's creepy sense of humor. One evening he dressed up as a ghost and "haunted" a group of men playing cards at his friend's house. When one of the guests rose from the card table and grabbed ahold of Edgar's nose to pull off his costume, Edgar fended him off with a cane while trying to avoid tripping over his sheet.

EN GARDE!

After he was finally subdued and unmasked, "Edgar laughed as heartily as ever a ghost did before," said one of the attendees.

It was clear that Edgar had a flair for the dramatic. To no one's surprise, he joined the local Thespian Society, where he and the other students put on sketches and plays under a tent erected on a vacant lot. They charged a penny for each performance.

Edgar Allan Poe was never the most popular kid in school. His gloomy disposition and odd behavior made him stand out in a crowd. And as an orphan suddenly transported to a new life in a new town, he was not the type to blend in right away. When he left home at age seventeen to attend the University of Virginia, he had already developed many of the traits that would help him become one of the nineteenth century's most celebrated writers of fantastic fiction: a deep love of poetry, a deathly fear of ghosts and monsters, and the theatrical panache of a master thespian.

SHERMAN ALEXIE

> ## Off the Reservation

G rowing up on an Indian reservation, where he
was bullied because of his health problems,
Sherman Alexie struggled to find a community he
could call his own. But a love of reading opened his
eyes to new possibilities of a life that lay beyond the
boundaries of "the Rez."

Shortly after **Sherman Alexie** was born, his parents received terrible news: their new baby had hydrocephalus, a serious medical condition in which fluid inside a person's brain causes it to swell and press against the skull. Sherman would need surgery. There was a chance he could die.

Sherman's surgery was successful. Doctors were able to relieve the swelling, though Sherman's head would always remain slightly larger than average. He also experienced side effects that lasted throughout his childhood, including bedwetting and seizures.

Sometimes these sudden attacks made Sherman feel like he had magical powers.

"The lights would pop, then I'd rise out of my body and be able to fly off anywhere I wanted," he remembered later. "I'd get to feel like a superhero for a couple of minutes."

WHOA, IS THAT <u>ME</u>?

But when the seizure subsided, he was back to being plain old Sherman Alexie—a poor kid growing up on the Spokane Indian Reservation in Wellpinit, Washington.

Sherman didn't mind living on "the Rez," as it was called. It was the only home he'd ever known, and he got to see things that kids from other cultures never experienced. One day, when he was a boy, Sherman stepped out of his house and saw a deer strolling through the center of town.

Another time, he watched a bear curl up and go to sleep on the roof of the town church. Respect for these creatures was an important part of the Spokane and Coeur d'Alene Indian culture that Sherman learned about from his parents.

Sherman liked to dream about what life was like outside the reservation, and that's where his health problems gave him a unique opportunity. Because his hydrocephalus required regular treatments in a hospital, Sherman spent long periods lying in bed with nothing to do but use his imagination.

One of his earliest memories is of his father bringing him a Superman comic that he'd bought at a local pawn shop. Sherman's father suffered from insomnia, so when Sherman was little, the two of them would stay up late into the night reading stories together. Sherman's dad liked mystery novels. Sherman preferred superhero comics.

By the time he was three years old, Sherman had moved on from comics to books. *Harold and the Purple Crayon* was one of his favorites. By age five, he was starting on adult fare, like John Steinbeck's *The Grapes of Wrath* and George Orwell's *Animal Farm.* His Grandma Etta—whom Sherman called "Big Mom"— would go shopping at garage sales and bring back stacks of books for Sherman to read. Sometimes they were romance novels for grown-ups or auto repair manuals. The subject didn't matter. "I just read everything," Sherman said later. "I wanted pages. Pages, stories. Anything."

By age twelve, Sherman had read every book in the reservation's library.

Sherman Alexie was now officially, in his own words, a "total geek." Unfortunately, being the town bookworm did not endear him to the other kids on the Rez, most of whom preferred taking part in traditional

Native American social gatherings, like powwows.

At school, Sherman was constantly teased by other kids. They called him "The Globe" because his head was enlarged from the hydrocephalus. They also mocked him for wearing thick glasses. Sherman had his nose broken five times because of fights he had with bullies. To avoid being beaten up, he spent all his free time in the school library.

The more Sherman read, the more dissatisfied he became with life on the reservation. One day, during math class, Sherman opened his textbook and found his mother's name written inside. He was so angry to see that his school was teaching from a thirty-year-old math book that he picked it up and threw it across the room.

Life on an Indian reservation was too close-knit, Sherman came to believe, because no one ever left. "I grew up in a house half a mile from the house where my mom was born," he once said. "When we have family reunions on the Rez, you just have to walk out the door and throw a rock, and you'll hit a cousin." In the sixth grade, Sherman created a family tree for a class project. He found that he was related to everyone in his class—including the teacher.

To broaden his horizons, Sherman decided that he had to leave the reservation. He enrolled at a public high school in Reardan, Washington. Sherman's new school was twenty-two miles away from the Rez. Because his family didn't own a car, he had to hitch rides with strangers or walk to class every day.

Sherman was the only Native American student at his new high school. But that didn't bother him. Not fitting in was something he was used to. He excelled at his studies and became a star player on the basketball team, which was named, oddly enough, the Reardan High Indians.

Sherman was an honor student, joined the debate team, and got elected class president. When he graduated from Reardan, he earned a full scholarship to Gonzaga University in Spokane. He later became the first person in his family to graduate from college.

"My flight across the reservation border was an outrageous and heroic act," Sherman later wrote. "Even now, I can't believe I had the courage to do it."

That act didn't just change Sherman's life. It provided the inspiration for his most famous novel. In 2007, after more than a decade of writing stories and poems for grown-ups, Sherman published his first book for young adults. *The Absolutely True Diary of a Part-Time Indian* tells the story of Arnold Spirit, a teenager born with hydrocephalus who overcomes his medical condition, battles back against the bullies at his reservation school, and finds his place among the bookworms and basketball players at an all-white high school.

Sherman Alexie's book became a best seller and won several prestigious literary awards. Apparently you don't have to be an Indian, or grow up on a reservation, to know what it's like not to fit in.

LEWIS CARROLL

One
Tough
Nerd

As an adult, the author of *Alice's Adventures in Wonderland* cut a less than imposing figure. Thin and frail, with a pronounced stutter, Lewis Carroll spent much of his time with his nose buried in a math textbook. But beneath this geeky exterior was a fearless fighter who never let a bully get the best of him.

Lewis Carroll's most famous character is a curious, brave, and intelligent girl named Alice, who relies on her wits to help find her way through a mad underground world populated by strange creatures. The real-life Lewis Carroll, whose name at birth was Charles Lutwidge Dodgson, shared many of the same traits as his fictional heroine. For example:

Charles was smart. It is said that he could read classical Latin by age eight. Charles's mother was in charge of his early education, drawing up lists of books for him to read and recording which ones he finished.

Charles was curious. Because mathematics was his father's favorite subject, Charles took an interest in it as well. One time, he found a book of advanced math in his house. He brought it to his father, pointing to a page of complex problems involving logarithms.

Mr. Dodgson informed his son that logarithms were much too difficult for a boy his age to understand. "But . . . please explain," Charles repeated, gesturing again to the page.

Charles was also brave. He was the third of eleven children, and the oldest boy. In nineteenth-century England, the firstborn son was expected to succeed his father as head of the family. As a result, Charles was protective of his siblings, especially the girls. Whenever one of his brothers or sisters had a problem, it was Charles who advised them how to deal with it. And when bullies bothered them, it was Charles's job to stand up to them.

That was difficult, because Charles was neither physically strong nor especially tough-looking. When still a baby, he had suffered a fever that left him deaf in one ear. Charles's eyes were not at the same level. One of his shoulders was higher than the other. Like all of his brothers and sisters, he stammered, making it hard for people to understand what he was saying.

For most of his childhood, Charles managed to avoid bullies. He grew up in a tiny village called Daresbury. His father was the reverend of a small church. Daresbury was very rural. There wasn't much entertainment. When a cart appeared on the road, it was a big event. All the local children would gather around to watch it pass.

The Dodgsons raised livestock and grew their own vegetables, and they had little contact with the world outside the parsonage walls.

When Charles was eleven, his father was promoted to rector of a new church in the village of Croft-on-Tees, in Yorkshire. The Dodgson family moved into a spacious church building with an opulent garden. This would remain their home for the next 25 years.

With more room to roam, Charles began to flourish. The rectory garden became his personal playground. Although he still spent much of his time lounging on the grass, reading math books, a whole new world of outdoor amusements awaited him. Charles made pets of the snails and toads he encountered. He even tried to coax earthworms into fighting each other, supplying them with tiny weapons fashioned out of clay pipe for their armed combat.

Over time, Charles's imagination grew wilder and his creative projects got bigger and bigger. He made his own train out of a wheelbarrow, a barrel, and a toy truck, which he used to carry passengers—his sisters, mostly—from one "station" in the rectory garden to another. At each station was a ticket window and a room to purchase refreshments for the journey.

Charles even wrote a long and complicated list of railway regulations for the passengers to follow. For example, no one was allowed to move around the cars while the train was in motion. Anyone who fell onto the tracks had to allow at least three other trains to run over them before they qualified for medical attention. The station master had the authority to put anyone who misbehaved in jail.

Theater was another of Charles's obsessions. He taught himself sleight of hand, donned a brown wig and a long white robe, and presented magic shows on a small stage that he constructed with help from the village carpenter. Sometimes he staged performances with a troupe of marionettes that he made himself.

Not even the arrival of winter could slow Charles down. When a blizzard made it impossible to play in the garden, Charles created a maze through the snow and dared his brothers and sisters to solve it.

And when it was too cold and dark to go outside, Charles turned to writing. With help from his siblings, he made a series of illustrated magazines filled with stories, poems, and sketches from his imagination. The first issue, titled "Useful and Instructive Poetry," included several of Charles's nonsense limericks. One is about a girl named Lucy O'Finner, who "grew constantly thinner and thinner":

THE REASON WAS PLAIN, SHE SLEPT OUT IN THE RAIN, AND NEVER WAS ALLOWED ANY DINNER.

But if Charles's poems and performances made him a star within his family, they did not endear him to his schoolmates. When he was twelve, Charles was sent to grammar school in the nearby village of Richmond. It was there that he had his first face-to-face encounter with bullies.

With his stammer and his thin, pale appearance, Charles was an easy target. Soon after his arrival, other boys began to play tricks on him. One time, they proposed playing a game called "King of the Cobblers" and asked Charles if he wanted to be king. When Charles agreed, the boys made him sit on the ground.

When he told them to get to work, they started kicking him.

Apparently, in this game, it was not so good to be the king.

Another time, some of Charles's classmates called for a game of "Peter the Red Lion." One of them made a mark on a tombstone; with closed eyes, the boy who was "it" had to try to touch the mark with his finger. When it was Charles's turn, he headed straight for the mark, only to poke his finger into a wet, clammy mouth. One of the boys was standing in front of the gravestone with his mouth open.

The boys probably thought that tricks like these would break Charles's spirit, but they were wrong. Or maybe they hoped to recruit Charles to the cause of tormenting their younger, smaller classmates. But the opposite occurred. Charles soon developed a reputation as a boy who stood up against anyone who mistreated others. By the time he left Richmond two years later, Charles Dodgson was, according to one biographer, "famous as a champion of the weak and small, while every bully had good reason to fear him."

NEVER FEAR, CHILDREN. YOU ARE UNDER MY PROTECTION.

The same thing happened at the next school Charles attended. Rugby School was an even harsher environment for a sensitive boy like Charles. Bullying was rampant. On cold nights, the older boys would steal the blankets off the smaller boys' beds, leaving them vulnerable to the chill. The boys who didn't take part in sports were mocked. Anyone who violated the school-

yard rules was made to write out an "imposition"—
hundreds of lines of Latin or Greek that took hours to
complete.

Injustices like these made Charles's blood boil. He
wanted to fight back, but his deteriorating health made
doing so difficult. In the spring, he contracted
whooping cough. Then he caught the mumps, which
worsened his hearing problem. And there was his
stammer, which marked him as different the moment he
tried to speak.

Because he could no longer confront his tormentors,
Charles got revenge in a different way. He outperformed
them in the classroom. He excelled at mathematics,
earning a steady stream of prizes. When Charles
graduated from Rugby in December 1849, the school's

math master crowned him one of the most promising students he had ever taught.

The next May, Charles traveled to the prestigious University of Oxford to begin his studies. The environment at Oxford was very different. There were no bullies, and Charles was again free to pursue his love of math, writing nonsense rhymes, and making up games and puzzles. Later, he would remember his years in public school as an unhappy time. Yet they reveal the inner toughness of the boy who became Lewis Carroll.

LAURA INGALLS WILDER

Heart
of a
Pioneer

The author of *Little House on the Prairie* based her classic novels on her own experiences growing up in a pioneer family. Life on the frontier was often harsh, but with each hardship, Laura grew stronger and took on more responsibilities. From insect invasions to raging blizzards, there was nothing this tiny trailblazer couldn't handle.

"My parents possessed the spirit of the frontier," wrote Laura Ingalls Wilder. Well, one of her parents did.

Laura's father, Charles Ingalls, had the heart of a pioneer. He never stayed in a place for long. He needed elbow room and quickly grew tired of an area as it became more crowded. Laura's mother, Caroline, preferred to stay settled in one place, but she reluctantly went along with her husband's wish to be constantly on the move.

By the time she turned seven, Laura Ingalls had moved three times. In fact, one of her earliest memories is of her parents packing all their belongings into a covered wagon for the trip from Wisconsin to Kansas when she was just two years old.

Like her father, Laura found changing places exciting rather than terrifying, even though the relocations often ended in hardship . . . or outright disaster.

Whenever the family moved, they traveled day and night, stopping only for meals. In the evening, they cooked corncakes and salt pork over an open fire. After dinner, Laura's pa would go to the wagon, unpack his fiddle, and entertain the family with a song or two by the flickering campfire.

ALL AROUND THE MULBERRY BUSH, THE MONKEY CHASED THE WEASEL

Although her sister Mary was the oldest child in the Ingalls family, Laura was Pa's favorite. Years later, Laura described herself as a tomboy who was full of energy and curiosity about the world around her. Pa nicknamed her "Flutterbudget" because she was constantly flitting about, looking for new projects that she and her father could get into together. He also called her his "little half-pint of cider half drunk up," or Half Pint for short.

After they arrived in Kansas, Laura helped her father build a house out of logs. One day, she saw Indians on the trail that ran past her house. That night she heard the sound of tom-toms in the distance.

The Ingalls did not know it yet, but they had built their new home on land that belonged to the Osage tribe. When they had arrived, the Osage were away on a hunting trip. But now they were back and surprised to find white settlers living on their territory. After being told of their mistake, the Ingalls family agreed to leave. Once again they loaded up the wagon and returned to the Big Woods of Wisconsin, where they lived for the next four years.

As more and more people began to move into the area, however, Laura's father started feeling restless again. He grew increasingly irritated at the sound of new settlers chopping down trees all around him.

Pa's dream was to live on a sprawling farm where neighbors were scarce and wild animals could run free. He heard about a town in Minnesota where there was plenty of room to roam.

After he had saved enough money, Pa bought a one-room dugout house in the town of Walnut Grove, Minnesota. The place was tiny, about the size of the wagon the family had just unloaded, but it sat on a parcel of farmland where he hoped to raise acres of wheat to sell to the big flour mills in the city of St. Paul.

In the fall, Laura and Mary started school. Laura was barely five years old, but the two-mile walk to the schoolhouse with her sister every morning was her favorite part of the day—even if they had to walk barefoot because their parents could not afford shoes for them.

The Minnesota winters were harsh, but the heavy snows provided the moisture that would make Pa's wheat crop grow. It was in the summertime that the family's problems began.

One day, just before the harvest, Laura was working in the field when a strange cloud darkened the sky. But this was no rain cloud. It was a swarm of locusts, a kind of flying grasshopper that attacks crops. One of the insects peeled out of the cloud and dove, striking Laura square in the back of the head. Then the others followed.

AAAAH!

Soon, Laura was covered in bugs. They clung to her dress and clawed at her skin. When she beat them off, they covered the earth like a carpet until there was nowhere to walk without stepping on them. They ate everything.

When the locusts finally moved on, the wheat field had been stripped clean. Her father lost his entire harvest. Meanwhile, Laura and Mary could no longer walk to school because the ground was blanketed with squashed bugs. Their mother taught them at home instead.

The next summer, Laura's father intended to try again with another wheat crop. But he didn't realize that the locusts from the previous year had laid eggs before they left. When they hatched, the bugs started feeding again. Once again, the farmland was decimated.

This second invasion convinced Pa that wheat farming was not for him. It was time to load up the wagon again.

The next stop was Burr Oak, Iowa, where Laura's parents took jobs as managers of a busy hotel. Laura and Mary helped by working in the kitchen and running errands for guests. One day, Laura discovered a bullet hole in the dining room door. When she asked a hotel worker how it got there, she learned that the hotel's previous owner had tried to shoot his wife while in a drunken rage.

To Laura, this was an exciting bit of local lore, but Ma and Pa weren't thrilled about raising their children in such a dangerous environment. When the hotel was sold to a new owner, who planned to turn it into a general store, they took that as their cue to move back to Walnut Grove. They got into the covered wagon once more.

Although the locusts had since departed, Charles Ingalls had lost his appetite for farming. He took a job as a butcher, then as a store clerk. He was glad to have a steady paycheck after years of struggling to feed his family. Laura returned to her old school, where she discovered that the independent, pioneering spirit she had developed during her travels made her a natural leader to the younger girls on the playground. Ever the tomboy, she enticed them to join in such traditional boys' games as Pullaway, Ante-I-Over, and a new-fangled sport called baseball.

Mary, who was older and thought herself wiser, tried in vain to rein in her sister's adventurous nature.

Once, when Laura was rushing out of the schoolhouse door to join a raging snowball fight with some boys, Mary grabbed her by the hair and tried to pull her back inside. "You're not going out!" she ordered. "I won't have it!" But Laura was too strong and dragged Mary outside and into the fray. They were both instantly bombarded with snowy projectiles launched by the boys.

Laura would have been content to go on being the "bad girl" in the Ingalls family. But then an unexpected crisis forced her to take on an important responsibility.

When Laura was twelve years old, Mary suddenly fell very ill. Her fever was so high that their mother had to chop off Mary's hair to keep her head cool. Doctors later determined that Mary had suffered a stroke. The illness left her blind.

Pa sat Laura down and explained that from then on, she had to serve as Mary's eyes. So Laura made a habit of looking at everything twice—once for herself, and a second time so she could describe what she'd seen to her sister.

The next time the Ingalls family moved, they left the covered wagon behind and traveled by rail. It was the girls' first train ride. As the big locomotive chugged to the Dakota Territory, where Pa had taken a job as a store manager, Laura narrated every aspect of their journey. She told Mary all about the other passengers: what they looked like, what they were wearing, and what they were doing. She also described the railroad workers as they toiled on the tracks.

The Ingalls bought a home in a newly settled town called De Smet. Laura enrolled in the local school. At night, she repeated all her lessons aloud so that Mary could keep up with her studies. Mary decided that she wanted to enroll at the Iowa College for the Blind, a school that helped blind people learn how to live independently. Laura was determined to help. She took a job in a dry-goods store to contribute to Mary's tuition.

By the end of the summer, Laura had saved $9 for her sister. That fall, Mary took a train to Vinton, Iowa, to begin her studies. The teachers were impressed at how well-schooled she was. Hearing about their compliments made Laura smile, for she knew that she had been her sister's primary instructor.

Laura was not the only one who made sacrifices. During one especially bad winter, a monstrous blizzard struck De Smet. The trains stopped running and everyone ran out of food.

One of Laura's schoolmates, Ed "Cap" Garland, and his friend Almanzo Wilder volunteered to travel twelve miles through the blizzard to find the one farmer who still had wheat left over from the summer harvest. They dragged sixty bushels of wheat back to town, using sleds that kept getting bogged down in the snow. They arrived just as another storm was about to hit. Their brave effort saved countless lives.

Almanzo Wilder's courage impressed Laura. And it would end up changing her life. When she was fifteen, Laura accepted a teaching position at Brewster School, twelve miles outside De Smet. At the end of her first week, she was told that she had a visitor. It was Almanzo, who had come with his sled and an offer to escort her home for the weekend. The trip became a weekly ritual. On one of those sleigh rides, Almanzo asked Laura to marry him. She said yes.

A short time later, the two were married. They bought their own "little house on the prairie" and Laura took on all the responsibilities of a homesteader's wife.

No matter where life took her, Laura Ingalls Wilder never lost the independent spirit that had enabled her to survive the rough-and-tumble years of her girlhood.

TWO

ALL IN THE FAMILY

SIBLINGS, PARENTS, GRANDPARENTS, AND ALL KINDS OF RELATIVES, THESE Kid Authors HAD A FAMILY MEMBER IN THEIR CORNER.

ZORA NEALE HURSTON

Jumping at
the Sun

Her folk tales of African American life in the
American South brought her fame, but Zora
Neale Hurston's proudest achievement may have been
educating herself at a time when opportunities for
black people were few. To do so, she relied on words of
inspiration from her mother, who always encouraged
her daughter to reach for the highest star.

"Always jump at the sun," Zora Neale Hurston's mother used to tell her. "You might not land on the sun, but at least you will get off the ground."

All her life, Zora tried to follow her mother's advice—as well as the example of Lucy Ann Hurston's sunny personality. Zora's name means "sunrise" in Slovak, but she was not of Slovakian heritage. She was an African American from Notasulga, Alabama.

The first time Zora jumped at the sun was literally the first time she jumped. One day, when Zora was still a baby, her mom left her alone on the kitchen floor while she went outside. She handed Zora a slice of cornbread to keep her occupied. Lucy Ann was gone only a few minutes when a wild hog ambled into the house. While the hog hoovered up the cornbread crumbs, Zora crawled to a nearby chair, hauled herself to her feet, and started walking for the first time.

Afterward, there was no stopping Zora from exploring. "Once I found the use of my feet, they took to wandering," she later wrote. "I always wanted to go."

Zora's father, John Hurston, did not share his wife's optimistic view. But he wanted to go, too—to seek a better life for his family. So in 1894, when Zora was three years old, he bought a house for them in the newly settled town of Eatonville, Florida.

Eatonville was very different from the town where Zora was born. Notasulga was segregated by race, which meant that black people were forced into second-class status by the white community. They weren't allowed to eat, sleep, travel, or learn in the same places as the white residents. Eatonville, by contrast, was an all-black settlement, a place where African Americans could run their own affairs—including the only school for black children in that part of Florida.

STRIKE HIM OUT, BOBBY!

John Hurston built a successful carpentry business, and Lucy Ann found work as a seamstress. It was in Eatonville that Zora learned how to read and make up stories. Using only her imagination, she could fashion a tale out of almost anything.

One day she fished an ear of corn out of the trash and named it "Miss Corn Shuck." Next she took a bar of soap off her mother's dresser and dubbed it "Mr. Sweet Smell." She found an old doorknob, which became, in her mind, "Reverend Door Knob." Finally, Zora borrowed some spools of thread from her mother's sewing machine and called them the Spool People.

Zora soon discovered a crawl space beneath her new house, where she played out her new friends' adventures. Like characters on TV, they went on trips together, attended fancy balls, and even married each other.

Zora found more inspiration for her storytelling in town, at Joe Clarke's general store. That was where the men of Eatonville gathered to gossip and swap tall tales—a local ritual known as a "lying session." When she was little, Zora liked to hang out on the front porch of Joe Clarke's and eavesdrop on their conversations. It was there that she first heard about Br'er Rabbit, Br'er Fox, and other characters from the African American folktales of Uncle Remus.

It was also at the store that she learned the many colorful turns of phrase that she would one day use in her writing. When the men were sad, they said, "I been in sorrow's kitchen and licked out all the pots." When they were happy, they declared, "I have stood on the peaky mountain wrapped in rainbows."

Zora's way with words began to attract the attention of other people, including those from outside Eatonville. When she was ten, two white schoolteachers from Minnesota came to town to observe the students in Zora's school. The women asked the children to read aloud from a book of Greek mythology. Most struggled to pronounce the names, but Zora read her passage perfectly. She had already read the book at home.

The next day, the schoolteachers gave Zora a prize for being the best reader in her class: a coin wrapper containing one hundred shiny new pennies.

They also presented her with a library full of books. This collection of fairy tales, myths, and folk legends— together with the "lies" she overheard at Joe Clarke's store—became the basis for many of the stories that Zora would one day write.

Inspired by the teachers' visit, Zora became curious about the world beyond Eatonville. When school was out, she liked to climb onto the gatepost outside her house and watch the white people pass by in their horse-drawn wagons. Some even drove what was then a new and fantastic invention called an automobile. If Zora was feeling especially brave, she'd clamber down and walk beside one of the slow-moving vehicles.

Sometimes the drivers would let her ride in the car for a while.

Zora's father didn't like her riding with strangers. In fact, he was skeptical about this whole "let your imagination run wild" business. He believed that his children should stay in their place and not mix with people from outside of town, especially white people. But Zora's mom thought differently. She knew Zora was just jumping at the sun again. "I don't want to squinch her spirit," she told her husband when he suggested that they punish Zora for her wandering ways.

It seemed like, as long as Lucy Ann Hurston was around, Zora would always be allowed to let her creativity roam free. But that changed the year Zora turned thirteen. Her mother fell ill and died, leaving her father in charge of Zora's education.

Zora's father decided to send her away to a boarding school in Jacksonville, Florida, which was more than 100 miles away. Jacksonville was a segregated city. White kids and black kids were taught in separate classrooms. Zora had to ride in the back of the streetcar to get around town. People in the general store didn't welcome her the way they did back home. Some even called her names because of the color of her skin.

IT'S BUMPIER IN THE BACK.

DING
DING!

CAPITAL 57 TRACK

The next few years were some of the most difficult in Zora's life. Her father remarried and lost interest in Zora's education. When he stopped paying her tuition, Zora took a job cleaning the school kitchen to cover her expenses. At the end of the semester, the assistant principal had to lend her money to pay her way back home.

Unable to return to Jacksonville, Zora could have given up on school entirely, but she remembered her mother's advice: "Always jump at the sun." She found work as a maid in the homes of wealthy white families. She never lasted long at any of these jobs because she spent more time reading than cleaning.

JUST ONE MORE CHAPTER, THEN I'LL FINISH DUSTING.

"I did very badly," Zora later wrote. "It was not that I was lazy. I just was not interested in dusting and dishwashing."

In time, Zora found a better job as a wardrobe assistant with a theater company. The troupe went on tour, and Zora got a glimpse of life beyond Florida. When they stopped in Baltimore, Zora decided to stay and enroll in high school. By working during the day and going to class at night, she was able to graduate in two years and win acceptance to Howard University, one of the country's most prestigious black colleges.

Lucy Ann Hurston never got the chance to see Zora complete her education, but it was her words of encouragement that inspired her daughter to do so. By urging her to leap past limitations, she made it possible for Zora Neale Hurston to soar.

I JUMPED AT THE SUN, MAMA, JUST LIKE YOU SAID.

MARK TWAIN

Bad Boy
Makes Good

Born under a lucky star—in fact, a streaking comet—Mark Twain survived a reckless childhood spent playing pranks, swimming in the Mississippi River, and exploring forbidden caves. But when his father died unexpectedly, this young Missouri-born mischief maker was forced to grow up in a hurry.

Shortly before Mark Twain was born, a dazzling streak of light blazed across the night sky over Florida, Missouri. It was Halley's Comet, and it would be another 76 years before it appeared again. Some would see the comet's appearance as a sign from the heavens that a great author had come into the world. But to his anxious parents, it must have seemed like a bad omen.

Samuel Langhorne Clemens was born two months premature. As a child, he was so pale, thin, and sickly that his own mother confessed, "I could see no promise in him." Everyone called him "Little Sammy" because he was so small and frail.

Sam's father, John Marshall Clemens, was a stern and unsmiling man who dreamed of striking it rich in business, but he rarely met with success. When Sam was four years old, the growing Clemens family moved to Hannibal, Missouri, a bustling port town on the Mississippi River. Sadly, his father's fortunes did not improve. Years later, Sam recalled that he had never once seen his father laugh.

Sam's mother was very different from his father. Jane Clemens was an extrovert. She loved music, dancing, and telling stories. Besides Sam, her second-youngest child, she gave birth to six more children and took in nineteen stray cats. Sam inherited much of his outgoing personality from her.

Because Sam was often ill and confined to bed, Jane forged a close bond with her son. She was indulgent toward him and would often look the other way when he got into mischief, which was often.

For example, when no one was looking, Sam liked to slip a tiny garter snake into his mother's sewing basket, then giggle as she opened the lid and shrieked in terror.

He also stole watermelons from neighboring farmers' fields and held seed-spitting contests with his brothers and sisters. One time, Sam bit into a watermelon that was not quite ripe. He was overcome by painful stomach cramps and nearly died of food poisoning.

One local landmark that figured prominently in Sam's boyhood adventures is the Mississippi River, which was just a block from Sam's house. Each day three steamboats docked on the riverbank. Sam would hear the ships' whistles blow and dream of one day becoming a pilot aboard one of these majestic vessels. (Years later, Sam would achieve his dream and get his famous pen name, Mark Twain, from a steamboat term meaning two fathoms deep—or twelve feet of water.)

When no boats were around, Sam liked to go swimming in the Mississippi, although it was strictly forbidden because of the strong currents. He nearly drowned on several occasions, but was rescued each time by the enslaved African Americans who worked nearby.

Sam's mother wasn't too worried about her son perishing in the river. She thought God had reserved a greater punishment for such an incorrigible child. "A person born to be hanged is safe in the water," she used to say.

As he grew older, Sam found cohorts in his hometown with whom he could share his escapades in and around the river. One of his closest boyhood friends was

Tom Blankenship. Tom went about unwashed, shabbily dressed, and always looking for trouble. Sam loved him like a brother.

Tom would climb the fence behind Sam's house and give the secret catcall that signaled the start of one of their misadventures. After Sam slipped out his bedroom window, they'd assemble the rest of their gang: schoolmates John Briggs and Will Bowen. If the weather was fair, they would play hooky and "borrow" a neighbor's boat to row out to Turtle Island. They'd spend the day there fishing, digging for turtle eggs, and smoking corncob pipes.

Sometimes the boys pretended to be Indians, or Robin Hood and his Merry Men, or treasure hunters in search of buried pirate gold. One of their favorite places to search for booty was a deep limestone cave.

The cave struck fear in the hearts of the towns-people. According to legend, a mad doctor had used the cave as a laboratory for hideous experiments on dead bodies. In his most macabre experiment, he reportedly tried to preserve the corpse of his own daughter inside a copper cylinder filled with alcohol.

It was also said that the Confederate Army had stashed weapons in the cave during the Civil War, that the outlaw Jesse James had signed his name on the wall, and that a local ne'er-do-well had gotten lost inside, surviving only by eating bats.

Sam told his mother about his visits to the cave, but she didn't pay much attention. Like everyone else in town, she knew that Sam was inclined to tell tall tales.

Sam could have continued like this forever, idling away the hours on Turtle Island or exploring McDowell's Cave. But then an unexpected tragedy steered his life in a different direction.

In 1847, when Sam was eleven years old, his father died of pneumonia. Now Sam was expected to find a job and help support his family. He landed work after school as an errand boy, a grocery clerk, and an apprentice to the town blacksmith.

After completing fifth grade, Sam dropped out of school and accepted a position as a "printer's devil" with the *Missouri Courier*. His job was to help the newspaper's proprietor set stories into type using a huge, unwieldy machine called a printing press.

It was grueling, grimy work and, worst of all, it didn't pay. Instead of a salary, Sam was provided with room and board, plus two suits of clothes a year. These items were typically drawn from the owner's own closet. The older man was twice Sam's size, so his hand-me-downs were comically ill-fitting.

Sam felt odd in the oversize clothing. The shirts "gave me the uncomfortable sense of living in a circus tent," he later wrote. "I had to turn up his pants to my ears to make them short enough."

Still, Sam persevered and learned the skills he needed to move on to his next job. When he was fifteen, he accepted an offer from his older brother Orion to work for the newspaper he now owned, the *Hannibal Journal*. The wages were scarcely better, and Orion often had trouble paying.

But Sam made the most of it. He started writing humorous articles, using the name W. Epaminondas Adrastus Blab. Once, when Orion was away on business, Sam published his own "special edition" of the *Journal,* poking fun at Hannibal's leading citizens. The stunt caused a sensation, helping to make Samuel Langhorne Clemens a household name in town.

Eventually, Sam decided that he had completed his apprenticeship and needed to see other parts of the world. When he was seventeen, he told his mother he was taking a job with a printer in New York City. Before she would give her blessing, Jane Clemens made him take a good-behavior pledge. Sam had to promise not to drink, gamble, or get into mischief.

Sam suspected that he would have a hard time keeping his promise, but he was eager to pack his bags and get to rambling. He never settled down in one city for very long. After New York, he traveled to Philadelphia, St. Louis, Cincinnati, and San Francisco, among other places.

Whenever he had a free moment—which was rare—Sam wrote home to his mother. "I am wild with impatience to move—move—*Move!*" he confessed in one letter. "Curse the endless delays! . . . I wish I never had to stop *any*where a month. I do more mean things the moment I get a chance to fold my hands and sit down than ever I can get forgiveness for."

Years later, after he became a successful author, Sam apologized to his mother for the reckless behavior of his youth—much of which he'd turned into stories for his novels *The Adventures of Tom Sawyer* and *The Adventures of Huckleberry Finn.*

"You gave me more uneasiness than any child I had!" Jane Clemens told her son, who was now known to the world as Mark Twain.

"I suppose you were afraid I wouldn't live," Sam said.

"No," she said. "I was afraid you would!"

LANGSTON HUGHES

History Lessons

When he was seven years old, Langston Hughes went to live with his grandmother in Lawrence, Kansas. With her help, he learned all about the history of his family and its place in the African American struggle for freedom. In time, he would earn a place in the history books—as one of America's greatest poets.

"You can't sit there."

The first time Langston Hughes heard those words was at a drugstore counter in Topeka, Kansas. All he wanted was an ice cream soda, but he was told that he could not order one at the counter, next to the white customers, because he was African American. At that time, law and custom segregated white people from black people throughout the United States.

Later, when Langston tried to enroll in elementary school, officials there turned him away for the same reason. They told him the school was for whites only. He would have to attend the "colored" school, blocks away across a set of railroad tracks. But when Langston's mother complained to the principal, and then raised a fuss at a school board meeting, they finally relented. Langston became the first—and only—black student in his class.

Segregation took a toll on Langston's family as well. His father, James Nathaniel Hughes, studied hard to become a lawyer. But in the early 1900s, African Americans were often not allowed to pursue professional careers. After he was denied a chance to take the bar exam, James Nathaniel Hughes grew increasingly frustrated and angry about racism in American society. One day, he walked out of the house and never came back.

The family later learned that he had moved to Mexico. Langston saw his father only once more as a child. In 1907, when Langston was five, his mother took him to Mexico so they could reunite as a family. Shortly after they arrived, a massive earthquake struck. The foundations of their house shook. Giant tarantulas scampered out of cracks in the walls. As the building crumbled around them, Langston's father carried his son outside to safety.

Right then and there, Langston's mother decided that Mexico was too dangerous to live in. She loaded Langston on the first train back to Kansas and never looked back.

Langston's mother had a hard time raising her son on her own. She took a series of menial jobs, but struggled to make ends meet. Eventually, she left for Kansas City to look for work as an actress, leaving

Langston in the care of her mother, Mary Patterson Langston.

At first, Langston wasn't sure what to make of his grandmother. A wizened old woman with stringy hair, she spent most of her time in a rickety rocking chair. Covered with what appeared to be a moth-eaten shawl, she looked to him like an elderly Indian squaw. In fact, she was part black, part Cherokee, and fiercely proud of her mixed-race heritage.

A college graduate, Grandma Langston refused any job that she believed was beneath her. But because she rarely worked, she never had much money. She couldn't afford to buy Langston new clothes, so he had to wear ladies' shoes. Dinner consisted of dandelion greens and salt pork—if there was any to be had.

THEY'RE A LITTLE BIG.

CLOMP CLOMP CLOMP CLOMP

Sometimes, to help pay the bills, his grandmother rented her house to students from the University of Kansas. While their rooms were occupied, she and Langston had to stay with friends and neighbors. That was hard, because no matter where you went to sleep, you never felt like you were truly at home. But Grandma would pass the time by sharing stories of their family history.

Grandma's first husband had been an abolitionist, part of the anti-slavery movement in the United States. He was killed trying to help John Brown lead a slave rebellion in the days leading up to the Civil War. The shawl Grandma wore was the bullet-riddled coverlet he had been wearing when he fell in battle.

THIS ISN'T ANY OLD SHAWL, SONNY!

During the Civil War, Grandma had worked as a "conductor" on the Underground Railroad, helping freedom seekers escape to the North. Her brother, Langston's uncle John Mercer Langston, was one of the first African Americans elected to Congress after the war.

One time, Grandma took Langston to the town of Osawatomie, Kansas, a hotbed of the abolitionist movement, for a special ceremony. As Grandma sat up onstage as an honored guest, President Theodore Roosevelt gave a speech and dedicated a memorial to John Brown, praising his campaign to free African Americans from slavery.

On another occasion, Grandma took Langston to Topeka to hear Booker T. Washington, the former enslaved man turned educator and author, who was speaking at the local auditorium. The hall was packed with about 3,000 cheering onlookers. Langston would later remember that it was the first time he had ever seen a black man as the focus of such attention. "I was very proud that a man of my own color was the center of all this excitement," he said.

Grandma's family stories profoundly affected Langston. So did the many books and magazines she shared with him. The local library was one of the city's only integrated public buildings. Langston spent as much time there as possible, devouring collections of poems and prose, African American history and mythology.

Every now and then, Langston's mother would visit him at Grandma's house in Lawrence. Sometimes he'd return with her to Kansas City to see plays and operas or to visit the library there. On one of these trips, Langston went to a blues club for the first time. The music gave him the idea to write his own poems and set them to the rhythms of the blues. For now, though, Langston did not write down his verses. He kept them in his head.

THE WAY HE'S PLAYING, IT'S LIKE POETRY!

When Langston was twelve years old, his grand-mother died. For the next two years, he lived with her friends, the Reeds. Then, when he was fourteen, Langston's mother sent for him. She had remarried and now lived in Lincoln, Illinois.

When Langston graduated from the eighth grade, he was elected class poet by a unanimous vote. That was odd, because he had never written a poem, except in his head. To prove that he truly deserved the award, Langston went home and jotted down sixteen verses praising his teachers and classmates.

At the graduation ceremony, Langston read his poem aloud to thunderous applause. It was the beginning of a long and illustrious writing career.

In high school, Langston wrote for the school newspaper, edited the yearbook, and began to write short stories and dramatic plays. One of his first published poems, "When Sue Wears Red," employs the blues rhythms that became his trademark.

Every day after school, kids would gather around Langston's front porch to hear him recite his latest poem or tell stories about the heroes he had learned about: Booker T. Washington and John Mercer Langston, Grandma and her husband, John Brown, the abolitionists, and the Underground Railroad.

Today, African Americans and all lovers of poetry look up to Langston Hughes with the same admiration as he once felt for those who inspired him. Besides his many collections of verse, he also wrote several books for children celebrating black history and cultural icons, from Booker T. Washington to Jackie Robinson.

Outside his home in Harlem, New York, Hughes planted a "children's garden," where kids could gather to share their own stories as they weeded and watered the plants. Even after he grew old and stopped writing poetry, Langston Hughes could often be found with his nose in a good book—in the children's section of the Harlem public library.

JULES VERNE

Castaway for a Day

J ules Verne was ahead of his time. Though he lived in the 1800s, his amazing tales of adventure predicted such modern innovations as skyscrapers, submarines, and spaceships. How did he do it? He used his imagination and drew on his boyhood experience of being shipwrecked on his very own desert island.

Jules Verne was always fascinated by ships. The descendent of seafaring navigators, he grew up on an island in the middle of the Loire River, in the bustling port city of Nantes, France. As a boy, Jules used to gaze out his window at the great clipper ships and three-masted schooners as they pulled in and out of the local harbor.

Jules dreamed that one day he might climb those masts and set sail for exotic ports of call. But he was shy, and lacked confidence, so he never dared to set foot on their briny decks. Until one day . . .

When Jules was about eight years old, he was strolling along the docks and noticed that the watchman assigned to guard one of the majestic three-masters had ducked into the local wine shop for a drink.

"It's now or never," Jules thought. Summoning all his courage, he clambered aboard the empty vessel and started patrolling the deck as if he were its commander.

The first thing that struck him was the smell. It was a heady mix of pungent tar and sweet spices—the ship's cargo. Jules proceeded to the poop deck, where he was overwhelmed by the odor of the ocean.

He looked inside the cabins, where the sailors slept when the ship sailed on the open waters. He peeked into the captain's quarters, then gave the massive wheel a turn. "I fancied the vessel was about to leave its moorings," Jules remembered later, "and that I, an eight-year-old helmsman, was about to steer it out to sea."

Jules never forgot his visit to the empty ship. When he returned home, he was even more determined to take to the open water.

Two years later, Jules's family moved into a new house on the right bank of the Loire. From his bedroom, he would peer through a small telescope at the passing ships sailing up and down the waterway. He vowed that he would hitch a ride on one at the earliest opportunity.

Jules discovered there was a man at the far end of the harbor who rented out sailboats for one franc a day. Together with his younger brother Paul, he pooled enough spare change to hire a single-mast boat for an afternoon. It was leaky, and the boys had trouble steering and working the sails, but they managed to sail out on the Loire and returned safely a few hours later.

ANOTHER SUCCESSFUL VOYAGE!

The next week, the brothers returned with another franc. This time they rented a boat with two masts; then another time they got one that had three. Each time, their clumsy craft took on water and barely made it back to port. And each time, Jules gazed with envy at the stately yachts that passed them by and thought: "Someday, I will sail one of those."

Before Jules could set his sights on his own pleasure boat, he had to learn one last lesson from the rickety vessels supplied by the harborman. So one day while Paul was busy with schoolwork, Jules decided to rent one on his own.

That turned out to be a mistake. The "sorry yawl," as he called it, had barely made it 30 miles downstream when a plank came loose. Try as he might, Jules could not stop the gushing hole. The boat began to sink headfirst into the murky waters of the Loire. Jules barely had time to save himself by swimming to a nearby islet.

Jules was shipwrecked, stranded on a deserted oval of shoreline covered in thick reeds. He thought back to stories he had read about famous shipwrecks, in books like *Robinson Crusoe* and *The Swiss Family Robinson*. Those characters spent months—years, even—living on their own, far away from civilization, subsisting on whatever food they could find.

In a strange way, the idea appealed to Jules. As he looked around, he began to contemplate his options for survival: Should he build a hut out of logs for shelter?

Or maybe rub two sticks together to spark a fire and send out signals calling for help?

No, he didn't like that idea because "they would be answered too soon, and I should be saved quicker than I wished to be."

Jules decided that getting food was his biggest priority. But how? All of his provisions had sunk to the bottom of the river. He didn't have a fishing rod or a dog to go chasing birds. There were no shellfish on the little island. He thought that maybe he could make a fishing line out of reeds, but what good would a few minnows do? He was hungry!

In the end, Jules's growling stomach won out over his desire to live the castaway lifestyle. As soon as it was low tide, he simply waded into the ankle-deep waters of the river and walked to the right bank of the Loire. He had spent only a few hours roughing it on his deserted isle and was home in time for dinner.

But Jules had finally experienced the kind of seafaring adventure he had always dreamed about. His afternoon on the Loire, "with its headwinds, its foundering and disabled vessel," was "everything in fact that a shipwrecked mariner of my age could desire."

Inspired by his long-ago adventures, Jules Verne later wrote *Twenty Thousand Leagues Under the Sea* and *In Search of the Castaways*. He published his novels under the banner Extraordinary Voyages, and the series contains 54 books in all. The stories are filled with travel exploits, technology, and places both real and unreal. Because of the mix of fact and fiction, he is known as "the Father of Science Fiction."

After becoming a successful writer, Jules was finally able to buy a large and sturdy boat of his own. With his family, he sailed to countries near and far, all of which inspired his literary works.

"I have sometimes heard the reproach that my books excite young boys to quit their homes for adventurous travel," the author once remarked. "This, I am sure, has never been the case. But if boys should be brought to launch out into such enterprises, let them take example from the heroes of my *Extraordinary Voyages*, and they are sure to come safe into harbor again."

THREE

THE WRITE STUFF

COMICS, LIBRARY BOOKS, AND CANDY SHOPS—BEFORE THEY WERE FAMOUS, THESE Kid Authors FOUND STORIES EVERYWHERE.

ROALD DAHL

The Boy Who
Loved Candy

How do writers find ideas for their stories? Sometimes just by opening their eyes and looking around. Even ordinary, everyday things and scenery can spark a person's imagination. Roald Dahl's childhood fascination with candy became the inspiration for his classic books *Boy* and *Charlie and the Chocolate Factory.*

Why did they have to put a candy store so close to the school?

Every day, as he walked home from class, seven-year-old Roald Dahl was inexorably drawn to the sweets shop at 11 High Street in Llandaff, South Wales. It wasn't enough just to look at it, or to know that it was there. He and his friends had to stop and drool over the glorious confections arrayed in the window. What little spending money Roald had was soon separated from his pocket as if by an unseen magnet.

Roald had to decide: Would he get an Old Fashioned Humbug, a gold-colored mint with a chewy toffee center; the Bull's-eye, an anise-flavored treat shaped like a musket ball; or one of the blisteringly sour fruit candies known as Acid Drops?

Then there were the candies for only the most stout-hearted consumers. Gobstoppers were huge hard candies that changed color as you sucked them. And since it took about an hour to finish one, they provided many opportunities for entertainment along the way.

Of the odd-smelling treat known as the Tonsil Tickler, perhaps the less said, the better. One of Roald's friends devised a theory that they were flavored with a chemical designed by grown-ups to make kids sleepy.

Roald's favorite was the sherbet sucker—a straw filled with sugary powder—and licorice bootlace. The trick was to suck out all the sherbet, then cap it off with the licorice. "The sherbet fizzed in your mouth," Roald later explained, "and if you knew how to do it, you could make white froth come out of your nostrils."

IT'S WORKING!
IT'S WOOOORKING!

Perhaps the only drawback to Roald's daily visit to the candy store—other than the prospect of a lifetime of tooth decay—was dealing with the shop's proprietor, Katy Morgan, and her two daughters. All three dressed in long, old-fashioned skirts and dingy, cream-colored blouses. Their hair was a tangled mess and they would shout if anything upset them, which was often.

To Roald, they looked like a gaggle of old witches, like the ones he read about in ghost stories.

Later, when he became a celebrated author, Roald liked to exaggerate the events of his boyhood. He changed people's names so they sounded more colorful. He also described people in ways that made them seem bizarre or scary. In his book *Boy: Tales of Childhood*, he calls Katy Morgan "Mrs. Pratchett" and describes her as "a small skinny old hag with a moustache on her upper lip, little piggy eyes, and a mouth as sour as green gooseberry." She wears a gray, grimy apron, and her clothes are stained with bits and pieces of whatever she's had for breakfast.

Mrs. Pratchett insists on sticking her greasy fingers deep into the jars to pull out sweets for her customers, whom she routinely denies a bag. Instead, she ties up the candy in one of the dirty old newspapers she keeps on the counter.

In Roald's version of events, he exacts revenge on Mrs. Pratchett by stuffing a dead mouse inside the Gobstopper jar—a prank he triumphantly dubs "The Great Mouse Plot."

Did this really happen? We may never know, but it sure makes for a good story.

The building that housed Katy Morgan's sweets shop is still standing, though the candies are long gone. If you go there, you'll see a plaque commemorating the site of "The Great Mouse Plot":

ROALD DAHL
13 Sept 1916 - 23 Nov 1990
BOUGHT HIS
SWEETS
HERE

That wasn't the only time Roald's sweet tooth inspired one of his well-known literary works. If you've ever read *Charlie and the Chocolate Factory*, then you know the story of Willie Wonka and his workshop. But did you know that this fictional story was based on Roald's read experience as a top-secret candy taster?

When Roald was thirteen years old, his mother sent him to a boarding school called Repton. It was mostly a dismal place, with a cruel headmaster who doled out harsh punishments for even minor transgressions. But one thing made the experience worthwhile: the school doubled as an undercover testing lab for a candy company called Cadbury.

In those days, Cadbury and its biggest rival, Rowntree's, vied for chocolate-making supremacy in Britain. Each company would send spies, posing as employees, into the other's factories to steal recipes and trade secrets. But Cadbury had one advantage over its competitor: the boys of Repton.

Every few months, the chocolatier sent Roald and his schoolmates a gray cardboard box containing twelve chocolate bars wrapped in plain foil. Each bar was filled with something different. Roald's job was to taste and rate each one on a scale of 0 to 10.

There was also a space on the form for comments. "Too subtle for the common palate," Roald wrote elegantly of one insufficiently flavorful candy bar. Even at his age, he knew how to turn a phrase.

In his idle hours, Roald daydreamed about what the Cadbury factory must look like inside—the enormous inventing rooms where laboratory workers in white lab coats mixed melted brown goop in giant copper pots, searching for the next great-tasting treat. He imagined what it would be like to work there.

"It was lovely dreaming those dreams," he wrote many years later, "and I have no doubt at all that, thirty-five years later, when I was looking for a plot for my second book for children, I remembered those little cardboard boxes and the newly invented chocolates inside them."

That book, *Charlie and the Chocolate Factory*, became one of the best-selling children's books of all time. And it helped make Roald Dahl one of the world's best-known authors. The story of an eccentric candy mogul, his elaborate chocolate-making operation, and a rival's efforts to steal his secret formula may have seemed fantastical at the time, but it was all grounded in the real-life experiences of the kid who loved candy.

STAN LEE

The Incredible Reader

I f you've ever read a superhero comic book, then
you know about origin stories. They explain
how the hero acquired superpowers. Spider-Man was
a high school student bitten by a radioactive spider;
the Hulk was a scientist bombarded by gamma rays.
And Stan Lee, the man who created those characters,
was a young boy fueled by the power of words on a page.

Stan Lee's origin story begins not in a secret laboratory or a school for mutants, but in a New York City hospital. He was born Stanley Martin Lieber on December 28, 1922. His parents, Jack and Celia Lieber, were immigrants from Romania. When Stan was eight years old, his brother Larry was born. The family lived in an apartment on the Upper West Side.

Stan's father worked as a dress cutter in the city's Garment District. When the Great Depression hit, Jack Lieber lost his job and spent most of the next decade looking for work. Positions were scarce during those lean economic times, even for a man with experience. He took whatever work he could find.

Frustrated by his inability to find employment, Stan's dad took out his unhappiness on his family. Stan spent many nights in his room listening to his parents argue, usually about money. With his sons, Jack Lieber grew stern and demanding. He ordered Stan and Larry to brush their teeth according to his exact specifications, telling them to make sure to wash their tongues every time.

As their fortunes declined, the Liebers' home became too expensive, so they moved into a smaller one-bedroom apartment in the Bronx. Stan and Larry slept together in the bedroom, and their parents shared a foldout couch in the living room. The apartment's only window faced the side of another building, so when Stan looked outside, all he saw was a brick wall. He dreamed of being rich enough to afford his own place with a window facing the street.

To escape from these dismal circumstances, Stan began spending more time reading. He almost always had a book in his hands, even at mealtimes. He read while he ate his breakfast, over lunch, and at the dinner table. His mother even bought him a stand with little clips on the bottom to hold his books while he shoveled food into his mouth. When he ran out of books to read, Stan would move on to the labels on the ketchup bottle or the back of the cereal box.

Between meals, Stan would sit on the living room chair with the latest Hardy Boys adventure and his favorite snack: a crust of rye bread smeared with butter. Other books he returned to time and again were the classic tales of Arthur Conan Doyle, H. G. Wells, and Edgar Rice Burroughs. The plays of William Shakespeare, with their grand and soaring speeches, also struck a chord in him.

Sometimes Stan's mom would ask him to read to her, which he always did in his loudest, most theatrical voice. On Sunday nights, the Lieber family gathered around the radio to listen to popular programs. These featured stars like the comedian Jack Benny, Edgar Bergen and Charlie McCarthy (a ventriloquist and his dummy), and the mystical master Chandu the Magician.

At school, Stan sometimes had trouble fitting in, but not because he was a poor student. On the contrary, he did so well that he was allowed to skip grades. As a result, he was always the youngest kid in class. Stan also suffered because his father didn't have a job. While most of the other kids' parents could scrape together enough money to send them to camp in the summer, Stan spent his vacations at home, with only his books to keep him company.

When he wasn't reading, Stan liked to ride his bicycle through neighborhood streets. He imagined that he was one of King Arthur's knights, galloping through the forest on a majestic white horse, or an astronaut on a spaceship about to blast off for the moon.

More and more, Stan began to think of himself as the kind of person who would grow up to write the amazing adventure tales that he liked to read. He had already tried creating his own illustrated stories, using stick figures patterned after the characters in newspaper comic strips like Krazy Kat and Dick Tracy.

But he was never very good at drawing. Words were the part that Stan liked, and no one was better at transforming words into exciting true-life stories than his hero, Floyd Gibbons. A correspondent for the

Chicago Tribune newspaper, Gibbons filed dispatches from war zones and exotic places.

Gibbons wrote a series of articles about his exploits in Mexico, following the trail of the legendary rebel leader Pancho Villa. He was wounded on a battlefield in World War I and wore a distinctive white eye patch for the rest of his life.

Stan loved to read Gibbons's swashbuckling stories of derring-do and imagine that one day he might follow in the great reporter's footsteps.

When Stan was ten years old, he wrote a letter to Gibbons:

"Dear Mr. Gibbons, I am a fan, I like your column."

A week later, Floyd Gibbons's secretary wrote back. Stan was thrilled.

"Dear Stanley, Floyd Gibbons has asked me to thank you for your letter. It was nice to hear from you." Stan was so excited that he ran to show the letter to his mother.

It didn't even bother him that Gibbons had not personally written back. Just the thought that his favorite living writer had taken the time to dictate a reply was enough to keep Stan excited for an entire week. Later, when he became a professional writer, Stan would remember the effect that Gibbons's note had on him, and he always responded to fans who wrote to him.

Stan knew for sure what he wanted to be when he grew up, but it took time before he worked up the courage to send away his own writing to be evaluated by others. Once again, a newspaper provided the opportunity he needed.

When he was fifteen years old, Stan entered a writing contest sponsored by the *New York Herald-Tribune*. Contestants were asked to summarize the most important news story of the week in 250 words or less. As Stan later recalled, he entered the contest three weeks in a row and won all three times, collecting $60 in prize money. It was the first time Stan saw his name in print, and it gave him the confidence to continue to pursue a writing career.

EXCELSIOR!

In high school, Stan got a job at a newspaper writing "pre-obituaries" for celebrities who hadn't yet died. He joined the public-speaking club, where he polished his talent for entertaining audiences. And he signed on to the staff of the school literary magazine, *The Magpie*, where he adopted his now-famous pen name.

One day, Stan noticed that a painter had left his ladder standing in the middle of the *Magpie* office. As a joke, he climbed the steps and scribbled "Stan Lee Is God" on the ceiling. The name stuck, and a future comic book icon was born.

A short time later, Stan went to work at a small magazine publishing company called Timely Publications. One of Timely's editors, Joe Simon, took Stan under his wing. Together with the company's art director, Jack Kirby, Simon created his own superhero comic book, *Captain America*, and asked his new assistant to help him write it.

None of them knew it at the time, but one day, in the not-so-distant future, Joe Simon's young protégé would

join forces with Kirby to create the Incredible Hulk, the
Fantastic Four, and the X-Men. Another young artist,
Steve Ditko, teamed up with Stan to create the
Amazing Spider-Man, the web-slinging teenage superhero who would become the face of a new company
called Marvel Comics. Yes, Stanley Lieber's life was
over, but the legend of Stan Lee was just beginning.

INCREDIBLE!

SPECTACULAR!

EXCELSIOR!

JACK KIRBY

STAN LEE

STEVE DITKO

BEVERLY CLEARY

Flight
of the
Blackbird

The creator of Henry Huggins, Ramona, and other classic children's characters grew up in a world filled with books—her mom even founded the town library. But reading didn't always come easy. Beverly Cleary learned to love the written word the same way kids learn to walk: one step at a time.

Few authors capture life from a kid's perspective quite like Beverly Cleary. Her books featuring Henry Huggins, his dog Ribsy, and sisters Beezus and Ramona Quimby depict the everyday adventures of kids going to school, dealing with parents and friends, and getting involved in all manner of mischief.

You might think someone with a talent for writing kid's books would have read a lot of them as a child, but that was not the case.

Beverly Atlee Bunn was born on April 12, 1916. She spent her early years living on her family's farm in Yamhill, Oregon, a town so tiny that it had no library. With so few books around, Beverly had to make do with what she could find in her house. One of her first "picture books" was a collection of Jell-O recipes. Photographs of colorful, jiggling, gelatin desserts always made her smile.

Or she would leaf through magazines, skipping over articles to focus on the advertisements and their colorful cartoon characters: a yellow chick who sold kitchen cleanser, a pair of smiling twins who loved Campbell's Soup.

Beverly's mother was a schoolteacher who believed that the lack of reading material was having a destructive effect on the town of Yamhill.

"There is entirely too much gossip," she declared one day. "People would be better off reading books."

Though she was busy with work, Beverly's mother found time to lead the campaign to establish a town library. She went all around Yamhill asking people to donate books and bookcases for the cause.

Eventually Beverly's mother was able to secure the space to house a small public reading room that was open every Saturday afternoon.

Beverly loved hanging out at the library. She loved sitting in the big leather chairs that people had donated.

But she wasn't able to enjoy reading because there were still no children's books on the shelves. The citizens of Yamhill had donated only grown-up books—mostly about farming or other topics she found boring.

So Mrs. Bunn started a new campaign. She wrote to the Oregon state library and asked if they had any kids' books to share. They sent over crates of them. Soon the Yamhill library was full to bursting with over 200 volumes, including the stories of Beatrix Potter and the fairy tales of the Brothers Grimm.

But Beverly barely got the chance to explore them. When she was six years old, her family's fortunes took a turn for the worse. Her father announced that they were leaving Yamhill forever.

Beverly's parents sold their farm and moved to Portland, the biggest city in Oregon. Portland had many libraries—one on every corner, or so it seemed—and each was well-stocked with all manner of books. Beverly was eager to dive in—if only she could crack the reading code.

That fall, Beverly enrolled in Fernwood Grammar School, a two-story brick schoolhouse that was just six blocks from her new home. On the first day of class, she met her teacher. "My name is Miss Falb," the stern-looking, gray-haired woman intoned. She pronounced it "fob."

"Why is the L silent?" Beverly wondered. But she had no answer, for as much as she loved books, she could not yet read on her own. She could only copy words into her notebook. When she looked at books at home, her mother would narrate the stories aloud.

Miss Falb divided the class into three groups. Bluebirds were the advanced readers. They got to sit in seats by the windows. Redbirds were beginning readers who had not yet reached the advanced level. They were placed in the middle seats. Blackbirds were the struggling readers. They sat all the way up front, by the blackboard, and received special attention—but not the kind anybody wants.

Beverly was mortified to be a Blackbird. She was given long lists of words to memorize at home: "shad, shed, shod…shut, shot, ship," and so on. Beverly came to dread the days when it was her turn to repeat the words in front of the class.

Many nights, Beverly burst into tears as she studied her word charts. "But reading is fun!" her mother would insist. Beverly replied by stamping her feet and throwing her first-grade reader to the floor in frustration. For her, there was nothing fun about reading.

Then, in the second grade, Beverly got a new teacher. Miss Marius was a gentle, kindly woman who took a different approach from Miss Falb. On the first day of class, she summoned Beverly to her desk. She had heard about Beverly's reading problems, and she wanted to work on them together. She handed Beverly a second-grade reader and told her to try to read it on her own.

Some of the passages in the reader were familiar to Beverly from her days in her mother's library in Yamhill. Fairy tales like "Rumpelstiltskin" were easier to follow than the stories of spinning tops and prancing ponies she had learned in first grade.

BOOYAH! STRAW TO GOLD! BAM! IT'S EASY!

Slowly but surely, Beverly began to pick up the ability to read on her own. But reading was still a chore to her, associated with those hated word charts. She had conquered her *fear* of reading, but she still hadn't developed a *love* of reading. That would come next.

In the third grade, in Beverly's own words, "the miracle happened." On a rainy day, when she had nothing else to do, Beverly picked up a book that her mother had brought home from the library.

The Dutch Twins by Lucy Fitch Perkins tells the story of Kit and Kat, a five-year-old brother and sister who live in Holland. They don't do much besides go fishing with their grandfather, help their mother with her housework, and drive a milk cart around their yard, but Beverly found their story impossible to put down.

She had always been fascinated by twins, ever since the days when she used to follow the adventures of the Campbell's Soup twins in the magazine ads she read as a toddler. And though Kit and Kat live in a far-off country that Beverly had never visited, she felt she could relate to their problems. When the twins describe falling into the icy waters of the North Sea, Beverly understood because she had once fallen into the Yamhill River and needed to paddle to safety.

Beverly spent all afternoon finishing the book and then began to read the sequel, *The Swiss Twins*. Her mother agreed to put off Beverly's bedtime so she could complete that book, too.

"It was one of the most exciting days of my life," Beverly remembered later. "I could read and read with pleasure! Grown-ups were right after all. Reading *was* fun." At last, the Blackbird had taken wing!

A short time later, Beverly heard about a contest, sponsored by the *Oregon Journal* newspaper, offering a free book to any child who could write a book review. Beverly was assigned a copy of *The Story of Doctor Dolittle*, which she liked even more than *The Dutch Twins*.

Beverly's review ran in the *Oregon Journal*, accompanied by her portrait, taken by the paper's photographer. Soon everybody in Portland knew who she was. Beverly became a school celebrity.

The next few years were exciting for Beverly. She spent much of her free time in the library, reading all the books she could find. In the sixth grade, Beverly became friends with her school librarian, Miss Smith, who encouraged her to develop her writing ability along with her reading skills.

One day Miss Smith challenged Beverly and her classmates to go beyond what they read in books and to invent stories of their own.

"Pretend you live in George Washington's time and write a letter to someone describing an experience," she instructed the class.

Some of the kids were baffled by the assignment. How could they write about something they had not read about and could not possibly have lived through?

"Use your imaginations," Miss Smith told the class.

Beverly dove right in. She drew up a letter to her imaginary cousin talking about how she had helped feed General Washington's army during the winter siege at Valley Forge. Miss Smith read Beverly's letter aloud to the class, singling it out for special praise.

Next, Miss Smith instructed the class to write an essay about their favorite character from a book. By this time, Beverly had so many favorite characters that she couldn't choose just one. She decided to include them all, writing an imaginary tour-de-force that she called "A Journey through Bookland."

I CAN'T PICK JUST ONE CHARACTER!

YAR, IT'S HAARRRRD.

BEVERLY'S A GREAT WRITER.

I KNOW!

Miss Smith was impressed by Beverly's contribution. She told her that she should write children's books when she grew up.

Beverly liked that idea, although it would be many years before she became a published author. Appropriately enough, her moment of inspiration took place in—where else?—a public library.

After graduating from college, Beverly—who was now married and known as Beverly Cleary—took a job as a children's librarian in Yakima, Washington. One day, a group of boys came into the library looking for something to read.

"Where are the books about kids like us?" one kid asked. Beverly had no answer. She turned to the shelf and picked up a book about a talking dog.

"What is the matter with authors?" she said to herself. She knew she could write a better book for kids.

Soon after, Beverly started on the first book in her Henry Huggins series. When it was published in 1950, Beverly was praised for portraying the life of an ordinary kid experiencing the usual challenges of growing up.

In 2016, Beverly Cleary celebrated her one hundreth birthday. Forty-one books after she first put pen to paper, her characters are as popular as ever. The little girl who struggled to learn how to read has become one of the world's most widely read writers.

LUCY MAUD MONTGOMERY

The Adventures of Story Girl

S he called one of her famous characters the Story Girl, portraying her as a Canadian ten-year-old with a knack for telling tales. But Lucy Maud Montgomery was the real-life Story Girl. And one of her best stories was also one of her scariest.

The Story Girl is the title of one of Lucy Maud Montgomery's books. The title character, Sara Stanley, is a motherless girl with a story for every situation.

Not many people know that Maud based the character of Sara on herself, or that some of the best-loved stories in *The Story Girl* and *Anne of Green Gables* were drawn from her real life. In fact, one of the chapters in *The Story Girl* is based on Maud's own encounter with a "ghost" when she was seven years old.

Just like Sara, Maud grew up without a mother. When Maud was a baby, her mother died of tuberculosis. Her father sent Maud to live with her grandparents, Alexander and Lucy Macneill, in the farming town of Cavendish, on the north shore of Prince Edward Island, Canada. Maud grew up in a large farmhouse surrounded by apple orchards.

Maud's grandparents were stern and humorless, with strict rules for how their new ward should behave. Because she was an only child, Maud spent much of her time playing with dolls or reading books in her room. One of her favorites was a guide to the Pacific Islands. She liked that the book was filled with pictures of native chiefs sporting, as she later put it, "the most extraordinary hair arrangements."

The fairy tales of Hans Christian Andersen also delighted her, and she was always fond of ghost stories. (More on that later . . .)

As she grew older, Maud progressed from reading about fantastical characters to making up her own. In fact, she had not one, but two imaginary friends when she was a girl. They were called "The Window Friends," and they lived inside the two large glass doors on the family china cabinet. Little Maud would gaze at her own reflection in the glass doors and imagine there were two different girls looking back at her.

She called the girl in the left-hand door Katie Maurice. Katie was a little girl just like Maud. They would talk for hours, sharing secrets, especially in the evenings when the fireplace had just been lit and the shadows bounced off the walls of the sitting room.

In the right-hand door lived Lucy Gray. Lucy was grown up, and Maud did not like her as much as she liked Katie. Lucy was sad all the time and told Maud dismal stories about her troubles.

Still, Maud always made time to listen to Lucy's complaints because she didn't want to hurt her feelings. For a while, Katie and Lucy were Maud's constant companions—and her only friends.

The summer after Maud turned seven, she made her first real friends in her new town. Two little boys named Wellington and David Nelson came to board at her grandparents' house and attend the local school. Well and Dave were about Maud's age, and they shared her love of make-believe. They were also good at building things. Together, the three friends planted a garden and constructed a playhouse in Maud's front yard. The treehouse had a door with hinges made out of leather cut from old boots.

Maud, Well, and Dave had one other thing in common: they all liked telling stories. Especially scary ones. The more Maud listened to their yarns, the more terrified she became. Well was especially good at telling ghost stories. On summer evenings, the three friends would sit on the porch steps in the back of Maud's house while Well spun blood-curdling tales about the mysterious "white things" that haunted the spruce grove below the apple orchard.

The way Well told it, a white thing had once spooked his grandmother when she left her house one evening to milk the cows.

At first, she mistook the wraith for Well's grandfather, but when she went back inside, she found her husband lying on the sofa where she had left him. He insisted that he had not been out of the house.

The kids started to call the grove the Haunted Wood, and before long it consumed their imaginations.

None of them would go near the trees after sunset, for fear of falling into the clutches of a white thing as it made its earthly rounds. But as autumn approached and the days began to shorten, they often found themselves on the grove's outskirts as twilight descended.

One evening, as the end-of-summer shadows lengthened, the kids were outside playing when Maud happened to glance toward the Haunted Wood.

All of a sudden a chill went down her spine—there, underneath a juniper tree, was what looked to be a white thing, in all its unearthly glory.

The three friends froze at the sight of the shapeless and floating object in the gathering gloom.

Dave spoke first. "It's Mag Laird," he whispered uncertainly, citing the name of a beggar woman the kids knew from their trips into town.

"Nonsense!" Maud replied. "It must be a white calf."
Well nodded in agreement—a little too quickly, Maud
thought. The indistinct figure hovering before them
really did not look anything like a cow. Only one thing
was certain: it was moving in their direction.

With a simultaneous shriek, the three friends took
off for the safety of Maud's grandparents' house. But
Maud's grandmother, who had been knitting in the
upstairs bedroom only a few hours earlier, was nowhere
to be found. They then tried a neighbor's house.

"A ghost! A white thing!" they cried. But the
servants, who were the only ones home at the time,
refused to believe them. Eventually, the kids managed
to persuade them to go down to the Haunted Wood,
armed with a pitchfork for protection.

NEVER FEAR
CHILDREN,
WE'LL TAKE
CARE OF
THE SPECTER.

A short time later, the servants returned unharmed.

"There's nothing out there," they reported. But the kids were not surprised. They were convinced that the white thing had vanished once it chased them away from the woods. They were just as certain it would reappear if they went outside again, so they stayed put until Maud's grandfather arrived with orders to march right home . . . and to learn the true solution to the mystery.

So what really happened? Here's how Lucy Maud later described the ghostly episode:

A white tablecloth had been bleaching on the grass under the juniper tree, and, just at dusk, Grandmother, knitting in hand, went out to get it. She flung the cloth over her shoulder and then her ball fell and rolled over the dyke. She knelt down and was reaching over to pick it up when she was arrested by our sudden stampede and shrieks of terror. Before she could move or call out we had disappeared. So collapsed our last "ghost," and spectral terrors languished after that, for we were laughed at for many a long day.

That was the last time Lucy Maud Montgomery ever encountered a "ghost." But it was only the first of many such tales the Story Girl would tell.

JEFF KINNEY

Stuck
in the
Middle

"I was never a wimpy kid," Jeff Kinney has said. "But I had my wimpy moments." In those moments, the overlooked middle child turned to the work of Judy Blume and other classic authors for the inspiration that led him to create the best-selling *Diary of a Wimpy Kid* series.

In Jeff Kinney's *Diary of a Wimpy Kid* series, the hero, Greg Heffley, is constantly bedeviled by his cool older brother Rodrick and his spoiled younger brother Manny. In real life, Jeff Kinney had three pesky siblings to deal with—each one seemingly determined to remind him of the special torments reserved for the middle child in a family.

Jeff's older brother and sister, Scott and Annmarie, were waiting for him when his parents brought him home from the hospital. In fact, Scott immediately pronounced the hefty ten-pound baby "a doorbell," the three-year-old's word for "adorable."

Jeff's younger brother Patrick came along three years later, meaning that Jeff was almost perfectly sandwiched between two warring camps. The daily competition to see who would be the first to use the single bathroom reserved for kids was intense.

It didn't help that Jeff considered himself the smart one in the family, which he reminded his siblings of at every opportunity. For revenge they played tricks on him. One time, when Jeff was seven, they pulled off an epic prank that went down in Kinney family lore.

School had just let out for the year and Jeff was looking forward to sleeping in on his first day of summer vacation. At the crack of dawn, his older siblings rousted him out of bed and told him that he was late for class.

"You slept through the whole summer!" they informed him. "You even missed our trip to Disney World!"

In a panic, a still sleepy Jeff scrambled to get ready for school. He was halfway out the door when he realized he'd been bamboozled. Call it "The Rip Van Winkle Caper."

Jeff hoped that things would change when Patrick was born. Maybe Scott and Annmarie would direct their practical jokes at their youngest sibling instead. But that didn't happen. Quite the opposite, in fact. Patrick quickly became the favorite son.

"My younger brother was the new cute one and my two older siblings were the teens," Jeff later recalled. "So I was somewhere stuck in the middle."

It seemed as if Patrick could do no wrong. One time their parents caught him drawing a life-size self-portrait on the pantry door. Jeff was so sure his brother would be busted that he could barely contain his glee. But Brian and Patricia Kinney thought the drawing was a masterpiece, evidence that he was the artistic genius in the family. They didn't even make him erase it. For years, Jeff seethed every time he passed by the pantry. He was sure that if he'd done that, he would have been severely punished.

Harassed by Scott and Annmarie, jealous of the attention lavished on Patrick, Jeff realized that life as the middle child was never going to be fair. Instead of looking to exact revenge on his siblings, he sought solace in stories about kids dealing with the same sorts of problems.

One day, Jeff went to the bookshelf and pulled out a novel by Judy Blume. *Tales of a Fourth Grade Nothing* told the story of a nine-year-old boy named Peter Hatcher, who had an obnoxious younger brother named Fudge. To Peter's consternation, Fudge never gets punished for misbehaving.

The story immediately struck a chord with Jeff, who liked the way the author used humor to describe real-life situations. He went on to devour Judy Blume's other books. *Freckle Juice*, the tale of a boy who whips up a concoction to give him freckles, was his favorite.

Jeff didn't always feel like reading stories that made him think of his own life. Sometimes he just wanted to escape into an imaginary world. For that, he turned to fantasy stories by J. R. R. Tolkien, Terry Brooks, and C. S. Lewis, as well as the stash of comic books.

There were war stories, like *Frontline Combat*, and tales of knights, pirates, and musketeers retold in *Classics Illustrated*. But Jeff's all-time favorite comic was illustrator Carl Barks's *Uncle Scrooge* series, which chronicled the adventures of Donald Duck's wealthy uncle on his travels around the globe.

Jeff's father encouraged his son's love of comics by cutting out strips from newspaper funny pages and taping them to the refrigerator. That was how Jeff discovered *Calvin and Hobbes, Bloom County*, and *The Far Side*, three of his favorite comics growing up.

At school, Jeff started to draw his own cartoons in a sketchpad. He took an art class and learned to draw the people and things he saw around him. Before long, drawing was all Jeff wanted to do. When the other kids were outside playing sports or swimming, Jeff would hide out in the school bathroom so the coach couldn't find him. If it got cold, he would wrap himself in toilet paper to keep warm.

SOMETIMES, TO CREATE GREAT ART, ONE MUST SUFFER.

By middle school, Jeff's pencil sketches were getting huge—literally. He drew immense four-foot-tall drawings that attracted the attention of his teachers. They started putting his work on display inside a glass case in the school lobby.

Patrick became Jeff's biggest fan. One day, without asking permission, Jeff's little brother brought one of

173

his sketchbooks to school and passed it around. The other kids were amazed at Jeff's realistic renderings of *Star Wars* characters. Some even offered to buy Jeff's drawings. But when Jeff found out what Patrick had done, he was furious. He didn't think his drawings were good enough to be put up for sale.

It was many years before Jeff worked up the courage to sell some of his drawings. In college, he spent three years sending his cartoons to newspapers, hoping someone would buy them. But all he got was rejections. "I realized that the problem was that I couldn't draw well enough," he admitted. "My drawings weren't professional grade."

Then one day Jeff hit upon the idea of creating a character based on himself as a child. He would present the boy's sketches and observations in the form of a diary. That way, it wouldn't matter if the drawings didn't look professional. He was inspired by reading a Harry Potter book. "He's brave, he's magical, he's powerful," Jeff said later, "and I wasn't any of these things as a kid, so I wanted to create a character who was more like I was."

For the next four years, Jeff wracked his brain trying to remember the details of his childhood. He spent hours on the phone with his siblings, writing down every funny story they could recall: all the pranks that Scott and Annmarie played on him, the fights he had with Patrick, and his adventures in school.

OH RIGHT, I FORGOT ABOUT THE RIP VAN WINKLE CAPER!

When he had enough material to fill a dozen sketchbooks, Jeff showed his work to an editor at a comic book convention. To his surprise, the editor told him his work was just what publishers were looking for. A short time later, Jeff signed a contract to write the first book in the *Diary of a Wimpy Kid* series.

More than ten years and a dozen books later, Jeff is one of the world's most popular authors. Over 180 million copies of his *Wimpy Kid* books have been sold. Jeff and his wife, Julie, even own their own bookstore, An Unlikely Story, in his adopted hometown of Plainville, Massachusetts.

No one is happier for Jeff's success than his brothers and sister, who know what an important role they played in making this frustrated middle child the writer he is today.

TRY AS WE MIGHT,
WE COULDN'T FIT EVERY

Kid Author

INTO ONE BOOK.

TURN THE PAGE
FOR SOME

FUN FACTS
ABOUT OTHER FAMOUS WRITERS
YOU MAY HAVE HEARD ABOUT.

When he was eleven, CHARLES DICKENS was sent to work in a shoe polish factory. His job was to glue labels onto the polish jars.

||||||||||||||||||||||||||||||||||||||||||||||||||||||||||||||||||||||||||||||||||||||||||||||||||||

When no one showed up to his birthday party, six-year-old F. SCOTT FITZGERALD threw a tantrum and ate the entire cake—including the candles.

||||||||||||||||||||||||||||||||||||||||||||||||||||||||||||||||||||||||||||||||||||||||||||||||||||

The unusual spelling of *Twilight* author STEPHENIE MEYER's first name was her father's idea. His name is Stephen, so she became Stephen + ie.

||||||||||||||||||||||||||||||||||||||||||||||||||||||||||||||||||||||||||||||||||||||||||||||||||||

ERNEST HEMINGWAY's mother dressed him in his big sister's clothes until he was five years old. She told neighbors he was her other daughter, Ernestine.

||||||||||||||||||||||||||||||||||||||||||||||||||||||||||||||||||||||||||||||||||||||||||||||||||||

LOUISA MAY ALCOTT was a very competitive athlete. "No boy could be my friend till I had beaten him in a race," she wrote in her diary, "and no girl if she refused to climb trees, leap fences, and be a tomboy."

BEATRIX POTTER kept a menagerie of small animals in her bedroom, including several mice, assorted rabbits, a hedgehog and some bats, a frog named Punch, a pair of lizards named Toby and Judy, and a fourteen-inch-long ring snake named Sally.

Mystery writer **AGATHA CHRISTIE** was a shy girl who had difficulty making friends. To keep herself company, she invented a set of imaginary companions known as "The Kittens," whom she would talk to aloud for hours on end.

Two famous twentieth-century authors, **HARPER LEE** and **TRUMAN CAPOTE**, were best friends growing up in Alabama. In fact, Harper used to protect Truman from bullies.

When he was a boy, horror writer **STEPHEN KING** sold stories to his friends at school—until his teachers found out and made him return the money.

||||||||||||||||||||||||||||||||||||||||||||||||||||||||||||||||||||||||||||||||||||||||||||

The creator of Sherlock Holmes, **ARTHUR CONAN DOYLE**, took the name of his famous consulting detective from a classmate at his school: Patrick Sherlock.

||||||||||||||||||||||||||||||||||||||||||||||||||||||||||||||||||||||||||||||||||||||||||||

Ted Geisel (aka **DR. SEUSS**) received permission from his parents to draw with crayon on his bedroom walls. Do not attempt this without asking an adult for permission!

When she was sixteen, poet **MAYA ANGELOU** got a job as a cable car conductor in San Francisco.

||||||||||||||||||||||||||||||||||||||||||||||||||||||||||||||||||||||||||||||||||||||||||||||||||||||

Had he not contracted tuberculosis as a child, **ROBERT LOUIS STEVENSON** might have ended up a lighthouse builder like his father. When his nurse read stories to him in his sickbed, he caught the storytelling bug and decided to become a writer instead.

||||||||||||||||||||||||||||||||||||||||||||||||||||||||||||||||||||||||||||||||||||||||||||||||||||||

As kids, the **BRONTË SISTERS** created dueling imaginary kingdoms. Charlotte and her brother Branwell called their make-believe realm Angria, while younger sisters Emily and Anne dubbed theirs Gondal.

||||||||||||||||||||||||||||||||||||||||||||||||||||||||||||||||||||||||||||||||||||||||||||||||||||||

Born into enslavement, **FREDERICK DOUGLASS** was forbidden to read or write as a child. He taught himself to read by watching other children, and he practiced writing on fences, brick walls, and sidewalks. When he was twelve, he saved enough money shining shoes to buy his own journal.

HANS CHRISTIAN ANDERSEN once tried out to be a ballet dancer, using his hat as a tambourine to keep time. His performance was so bizarre, the ballerina for whom he was auditioning decided that he was a lunatic and had him thrown out of her house.

||||||||||||||||||||||||||||||||||||||||||||||||||||||||||||||||||||||||||||||||||||||||||||||||||||||||

Mary Wollstonecraft—who grew up to become *Frankenstein* author **MARY SHELLEY**—hated playing with dolls. She preferred to climb the ancient beech trees that grew on her family's property and spent hours staring up at the clouds.

||||||||||||||||||||||||||||||||||||||||||||||||||||||||||||||||||||||||||||||||||||||||||||||||||||||||

Poet **T. S. ELIOT** is a direct descendent of three American presidents: John Adams, John Quincy Adams, and Rutherford B. Hayes.

||||||||||||||||||||||||||||||||||||||||||||||||||||||||||||||||||||||||||||||||||||||||||||||||||||||||

RICHARD WRIGHT sold his first short story when he was just fifteen years old.

||||||||||||||||||||||||||||||||||||||||||||||||||||||||||||||||||||||||||||||||||||||||||||||||||||||||

VIRGINIA WOOLF was crazy about animals. As a girl growing up in London, she surrounded herself with an unusual menagerie that included a squirrel, a pygmy marmoset, and a pet mouse named Jacobi.

CHARLES SCHULZ had a dog named Spike that ate money, pins, tacks, and other inedible objects. At age 15, Schulz drew a sketch of the dog and submitted it to the newspaper comic "Ripley's Believe It or Not," which printed his illustration on February 22, 1937. It was Schulz's first published cartoon.

When he was a baby, **RALPH ELLISON**'s favorite food was steak and onions.

WILLIAM FAULKNER was a terrible student. One of his classmates called him "the laziest boy I ever saw . . . he would do nothing but write and draw."

When he was seven, **H. G. WELLS** broke his leg in an accident and spent several months in bed reading every book he could get his hands on.

When she was eight years old, future *Color Purple* author **ALICE WALKER** was accidentally shot in the eye with a BB gun by her older brother during a game of Cowboys and Indians.

One of ten-year-old **DANIEL "LEMONY SNICKET" HANDLER**'s first stories was about a man who gets eaten alive by the leaves falling off a tree. "My teacher was horrified," Handler later said, "but I knew instantly that I'd written something good."

Science-fiction author **RAY BRADBURY** was inspired to become a writer after a carnival magician named Mr. Electrico reached out to him from the stage, touched him on the head with his sword, and commanded him to "Live forever!" "I decided that was the greatest idea I had ever heard," Bradbury said later. "I started writing every day. I never stopped."

Horror writer **H. P. LOVECRAFT** was so pale and sickly when he was a kid that his own mother ordered him to stay inside so no one could see him.

||||||||||||||||||||||||||||||||||||||||||||||||||||||||||||||||||||||||||||||||||||||||||||||||||||||||||||||

C. S. LEWIS never liked his first name (Clive). When he was four, he began insisting that all his friends call him Jack after his dog Jacksie.

||||||||||||||||||||||||||||||||||||||||||||||||||||||||||||||||||||||||||||||||||||||||||||||||||||||||||||||

When **SHEL SILVERSTEIN** was growing up, he wanted to be either a baseball player or popular with girls. But he was terrible at sports and girls did not like him, so he began to draw and write instead.

Further Reading

DO YOU KNOW WHERE THE CHEESE SECTION IS?

Bibliography

There are many great books about great authors, including autobiographies (books written by the person about himself or herself) and biographies (books about noteworthy people written by someone else). The following is a list of main sources used by the author in researching and writing this book.

PART ONE

It's Not Easy Being a Kid

J. R. R. Tolkien

Carpenter, Humphrey. *J. R. R. Tolkien: A Biography*. Boston: Houghton Mifflin, 2000.

Hammond, Wayne G., and Christina Scull. *J. R. R. Tolkien: Artist and Illustrator*. Mariner Books, 2000.

Neimark, Anne E. *Mythmaker: The Life of J. R. R. Tolkien*. Boston: Houghton Mifflin Harcourt, 2012.

Pearce, Joseph. *Tolkien: Man and Myth*. San Francisco: Ignatius Press, 1998.

J. K. Rowling

Pollack, Pam, and Meg Belviso. *Who Is J. K. Rowling?* New York: Grosset & Dunlap, 2012.

Rice, Dona Herweck. *Game Changers: A Biography of J. K. Rowling.* Teacher Created Materials. 2017.

Shapiro, Marc. *J. K. Rowling: The Wizard Behind Harry Potter.* New York: St. Martin's Press, 2007.

Edgar Allan Poe

Gigliotti, Jim, and Tim Foley. *Who Was Edgar Allan Poe?* Grosset & Dunlap, 2015.

Ackroyd, Peter. *Poe: A Life Cut Short.* New York: Doubleday, 2008.

Meyers, Jeffrey. *Edgar Allan Poe: His Life and Legacy.* New York: Cooper Square Press, 2000.

Sherman Alexie

Peterson, Nancy J. *Conversations with Sherman Alexie.* Jackson: University Press of Mississippi, 2009.

Sonneborn, Liz. *Sherman Alexie.* New York: Rosen Publishing Group, 2013.

Lewis Carroll

Carpenter, Angelica Shirley. *Lewis Carroll: Through the Looking Glass.* Lerner Publications, 2003.

Cohen, Morton N. *Lewis Carroll: A Biography.* New York: Vintage Books, 1995.

Woolf, Jenny. *The Mystery of Lewis Carroll.* New York: St. Martin's Griffin, 2010.

Laura Ingalls Wilder

Anderson, William. *Laura Ingalls Wilder: A Biography.* New York: HarperCollins, 1992.

Ford, Carin T. *Laura Ingalls Wilder: Real-Life Pioneer of the "Little House" Books.* Berkley Heights, N.J.: Enslow, 2003.

Gormley, Beatrice, and Meryl Henderson. *Laura Ingalls Wilder: Young Pioneer.* Aladdin, 2001.

PART TWO

All in the Family

Zora Neale Hurston

Bagge, Peter. *Fire!!: The Zora Neale Hurston Story.* Drawn and Quarterly, 2017.

Boyd, Valerie. *Wrapped in Rainbows: The Life of Zora Neale Hurston.* New York: Scribner, 2003.

Fradin, Dennis Brindell, and Judith Bloom Fradin. *Zora! The Life of Zora Neale Hurston.* Boston: Clarion Books, 2012.

Hurston, Zora Neale. *Dust Tracks on a Road.* New York: Harper Perennial, 1996.

Mark Twain

North, Sterling. *Mark Twain and the River.* New York: Puffin, 2009.

Powers, Ron. *Dangerous Waters: A Biography of the Boy Who Became Mark Twain.* New York: Da Capo, 1999.

————. *Mark Twain: A Life.* New York: Free Press, 2005.

Rasmussen, R. Kent. *Mark Twain for Kids.* Chicago Review Press, 2004.

Langston Hughes

Anthony, David H., and Stephanie Kuligowski. *Langston Hughes: Harlem Renaissance Writer.* Teacher Created Materials, 2011.

Cooper, Floyd. *Coming Home: From the Life of Langston Hughes.* New York: Putnam & Grosset, 1994.

Hughes, Langston. *The Big Sea.* New York: Knopf, 1940.

Rampersad, Arnold. *The Life of Langston Hughes.* New York: Oxford University Press, 1986.

Jules Verne

Butcher, William. *Jules Verne: The Definitive Biography.* New York: Thunder's Mouth Press, 2006.

Lottman, Herbert R. *Jules Verne: An Exploratory Biography.* New York: St. Martin's Press, 1996.

Schoell, William. *Remarkable Journeys: The Story of Jules Verne.* Greensboro, N.C.: Morgan Reynolds Publishing, 2002.

Streissguth, Tom. *Science Fiction Pioneer: A Story about Jules Verne.* Carolrhoda Books, 2000.

PART THREE

The Write Stuff

Roald Dahl

Dahl, Roald. *Boy: Tales of Childhood*. New York: Farrar, Straus, & Giroux, 1984.

Sturrock, Donald. *Storyteller: The Authorized Biography of Roald Dahl*. New York: Simon & Schuster, 2010.

Treglown, Jeremy. *Roald Dahl: A Biography*. New York: Farrar, Straus & Giroux, 1994.

Stan Lee

Lee, Stan, and George Mair. *Excelsior! The Amazing Life of Stan Lee*. New York: Simon & Schuster, 2002.

Lee, Stan, Peter David, and Colleen Doran. *Amazing Fantastic Incredible: A Marvelous Memoir*. New York: Simon & Schuster, 2015.

Raphael, Jordan, and Tom Spurgeon. *Stan Lee and the Rise and Fall of the American Comic Book*. Chicago: Chicago Review Press, 2003.

Beverly Cleary

Cleary, Beverly. *A Girl from Yamhill: A Memoir*. New York: Avon Books, 1988.

Foster, Laura. *Walking with Ramona: Exploring Beverly Cleary's Portland*. Microcosm Publishing, 2016.

Lucy Maud Montgomery

Heilbron, Alexandra. *Remembering Lucy Maud Montgomery*. Toronto: Dundurn Press, 2001.

Rubio, Mary Henley. *Lucy Maud Montgomery: The Gift of Wings*. Toronto: Anchor Canada, 2008.

Wallner, Alexandra. *Lucy Maud Montgomery*. Holiday House, 2006.

Jeff Kinney

Kinney, Patrick. *Who Is Jeff Kinney?* New York: Grosset & Dunlap, 2015.

Index

They're Little Kids with Big Dreams... and Big Problems!

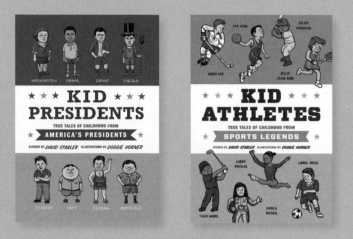